ELEVATION REQUIRES CHANGE

The Journey Towards Purpose and Fulfillment

DIMYAS PERDUE

Elevation Requires Change
The Journey Towards Purpose and Fulfillment

© 2023, Dimyas Perdue.

Print ISBN: 979-8-35090-097-2
eBook ISBN: 979-8-35090-098-9

Contents

A Letter From My Bride

MY DEAREST DIMYAS,

The time has come for the world to be blessed with your voice, your gifts, and your leadership. This journey to purpose and fulfillment has been a beautiful road in what we call life. The highs and the lows have brought you to where you are. The tragedies and triumphs have unlocked the greatness within you.

I am so grateful to bear witness to your writing through the rain. I am so blessed to hear your funny jokes which bring laughter and joy each and every day. I am honored to be your bride, mother to your children, and best friend for life. Thank you for being authentically you.

There is so much power in this book. There is so much power in your words. Each section speaks to so many walks of life. My hope is that each human being gains value from reading your words and passes it on to another. My vision is that you continue to grow, continue to write, and continue to transform lives for the better.

You are extraordinary, you are powerful, and your time is now.

With all my love and affection and with every part of my being I am so proud of you.

Love Always,
Piggy

Acknowledgements

WRITING THIS BOOK has been an incredible journey but it could not have happened without the support of my family and closest friends.

To my beautiful mother, Mrs. Edwina Relf, you are my world. I truly would not be here if it were not for you. Thank you for every meal, every talk, every kiss, and every hug. Oh, and every punishment too. God knows I deserved them.

Thank you for being the example of what a parent should be. In raising me the way you did, you raised your grandchildren. Thank you for never giving up on me. Thank you for praying for me. Thank you for teaching where my help comes from and helping me become the man of God I am today. I love you more than I will ever be able to show.

To my bride, Mrs. Jaimie Perdue, where do I start? Thanking you for your support over the years could be a book by itself. I am such a better man, father, friend, and husband because of you. Thank you for pushing me to be the best version of me. Thank you for not allowing me to accept less. Thank you for being an incredible mother to our children. Thank you for making me a better communicator. Thank you for helping me see my "sensitive" side. Thank you for taking off work to go through the book, provide insight, red pen, highlight, and edit. Thank you for booking the time away so I could leave and be in a place where creating this book was possible without distraction. Thank you for holding down the fort in my absence. I could not be here without you. You are my heartbeat. I love you now, I love you tomorrow, I love you forever.

To my Auntie, Patrice Obi, thank you. I don't know how you found me that day but you did. Thank you for stepping in and providing me with the tough love that gave me the rudder steers necessary to navigate life's rough waters. Had it not been for that conversation that night, and for the many other talks, this message to you would look a lot different. You have always been a voice of reason and the glue that kept us all so close. I love you and I am forever grateful.

To my Grandmother, The Matriarch, you are incredible. You are the epitome of resilience, perseverance, love, courage, and strength. Thank you for enduring. Thank you for giving all of yourself to your children and grandchildren. Thank you for the many lessons that echo in my mind daily. Thank you for always being present in my life. Thank you for all of the conversations throughout my professional career. I love you with all of my heart.

To my beautiful children, Dimyas Perdue II, Keimya Perdue, Kortni Perdue, Roman Perdue, Royal Perdue, and Royal Perdue II, where do I begin? I have done many great things in my life that fill me with pride but they can't compare to the pride I have in being your father. You have made me better. You have made me a better thinker. A better listener. A better speaker and most importantly, a better father. You have supported me through many things and have endured long periods of absence due to the career I chose and for this I say thank you.

For your entire life I have tried to set the example of what right looks like for you. To show you that it is ok to go off the beaten path. To let you see that it is ok not to do what everyone else does. I have also taught you to seek God in everything you do. And while I constantly try to be your earthly moral compass, my prayer is that you continue to seek God in everything you do so that your path is forever illuminated by the true source of light. I love you with every fiber of my being.

Horace Mann, in his address at Antioch College, said, "Be ashamed to die until you have won some victory for humanity." My goal with this book is to be able to leave a tool for all humankind to use long after I am gone. My victory for humanity before I die would be to help everyone that reads, hears, and acts on the ideas in this book to elevate to levels they never could have imagined. I truly hope you enjoy reading this book as much as I have enjoyed writing it.

1

The Letter That Changed Everything

DEAR DIMYAS,

So you're just going to lay there and act like you didn't make me a promise? You know there's no way I can do this by myself, and you keep telling me, "I got you" and that "we will do it tomorrow." Yet it seems to me like everything else and everyone else is far more important to you than I am. They mean more to you than I do, and clearly, they are worth more because they are who you spend your time with. When you decided this was what you wanted, I was all in. There was no doubt in my mind. You convinced me. You wrote me notes as a constant reminder that we would always be your top priority. You told me all I needed to do was be patient and everything I ever wanted us to be would come to fruition. When you woke up, I was the first thing on your mind. You daydreamed about me all day, and before you closed your eyes at night, it was me who captured your thoughts. And now, the entire day is gone and once again I am left feeling as if what you're telling me isn't what will be. I cannot help but wonder how many others you've left feeling this way.

Love always, despite everything,
Your Goals

2

Introduction

I CAN ONLY IMAGINE what you were thinking reading that letter. Midway through it you were probably asking yourself, "Is this some type of relationship drama?" Well to be honest, it is. It is a true description of what it has been like for me personally when it came to the things I told myself I wanted to accomplish. It is a depiction of the broken relationship I had in the past, where my efforts to attain my goal didn't measure up to what was needed to reach them. It was a love-hate relationship, but one that I could not run from any longer. Although this is a personal letter from my goals to me, if you're honest with yourself, you might see that the letter also applies to you. And if it doesn't, I am sure your goals might have a letter or two to write to you as well.

I thought a good way to start this book would be with that note to myself. I wrote it years ago, and when I read it the second time around, it hit me and convicted me more than anything else had in a long time. One of the main reasons it impacted me so much was that I was still in the same place. I realized what I had been doing for the longest time was making sure that what everyone else wanted me to do was done. If there was a last-minute meeting I needed to attend, I put aside my own priorities and went. If I had a friend dealing with an issue, I would rush to their side to assist, telling myself they were more important. Now, I'm not saying there is anything wrong with being there for others or attending last minute meetings. I'm merely noting the pattern of what I did and the effects of those actions. To put it into perspective,

I told myself five years ago I wanted to become a published author. Well, for five years I didn't accomplish it. I got a partial product. I got a partial product because I didn't put in the effort it would take to get a full product.

What made the difference for me was deciding I would do whatever it took to reconcile the relationship I had with setting and accomplishing my goals. There were too many occasions after keynotes or other lectures when other professionals would ask me, "Do you have a book?" To which I would reply, "It's in the works." Each time I would say that it would sting that much more knowing I had not done what I promised myself I would do.

I must admit, changing the behavior was not easy, and I was not always consistent. On countless occasions, I would start and stop before making any significant progress. I knew I needed to be consistent, so I did. What saddens me is how many others don't even get that far. They continue making excuses. They say they're too busy, or not motivated, or worse, they play on their life's misfortunes in an attempt to gain favor from others to cover their unwillingness to start and more importantly, finish.

So, what's at stake? Well, that depends on what you've set as being your mountain top. If it's quitting your job and starting the business you've dreamed of for years, what's at stake is an unfulfilled life. If it is making more time to be a better parent, what's at stake is having to look back after your working career is done and seeing children that have made their lives and personal agendas a priority over you, just as you did with them. If it is transforming your mind and your body, what's at stake is you never gaining the self-confidence you truly desire. No matter what it is, if you truly want it, the reasons why you can't do it need to become less than the reasons you can. It is time to separate yourself from your excuses, lace up your boots, and get ready to work.

One of the many reasons I decided to write this book is that I know I am not alone when it comes to having made and broken promises to myself. Many of you have or had this same non-committed relationship in the past with something you said you wanted in life. We've allowed other things to get in our way. Many times, it's not other *things* that have been in our way, but us standing in our own way. When we haven't accomplished what we said we wanted, oftentimes we try to point fingers at everyone else when in reality, the real enemy to my progression is the inner me.

For others of us, with the day-to-day hustle and bustle of our jobs and our families, we can easily find ourselves putting *self* on the backburner for the sake of tackling what is right in front of us. We do this because we care about the people we are working with and we care about our families, and we want to keep those relationships strong. Well, what about the relationship with yourself? How long will you continue to deny yourself what it is you truly want? How long will you continue to put this relationship in second place?

Millions of people all over the world put off their personal goals for one reason or another, and what's worse, many will never attempt to reconcile that relationship between setting goals and accomplishing them. For me, learning to make my goals a priority was a part of reconciling that relationship. With this book, my goal is to help you do the same. Life is a journey full of many twists and turns, ups and downs, and it is better done with a guide. It is my hope that this book and the motive behind its development will be a lantern that guides you through the darkness and aids in fulfilling your life's purpose.

Whether your goal is to accomplish something specific or to become a better person, doing it is going to take a lot more than just the desire. It is going to take work and focus for you to be able to get it done, and not everyone is willing to make that type of commitment. In order to get things done, it is important to remove all of the outside factors that prevent you from focusing. Sometimes that factor may be your friends. Other times it can be a busy work schedule that leaves you so tired that you don't want to do anything but sleep when you get home. No matter what has prevented you from striving towards your goals, in the journey towards purpose and fulfillment, nothing can continue to stand in your way once you make the decision to dream again.

3

Dare to Dream

ONE OF THE greatest dreams ever spoken out loud was delivered in front of a nation of people during a time of turmoil and chaos. It was a dream that would face adversity, challenge, and carry with it the risk of hurt, harm, and death every day. Despite everything that was opposed to it, the dream of Dr. Martin Luther King Jr. went from a figment of his imagination to a reality for us all. It didn't happen just because he spoke it. It came true through his faith, his work, and on the shoulders of those who put their lives on the line so that the injustices of that day would no longer be commonplace in our society.

It took courage during the civil rights movement to stand up day in and day out, and the same type of courage will be required of you as you pursue greatness. It's the courage and daring to dream. To dream of standing on your mountain top. Just as Dr. King and those who stood beside him weren't great in number, the truth is, the number of those who are willing to take a chance on themselves aren't great either. Not everyone is willing to do it. Why do you think that is? I mean, every child grows up wanting to be something. For me, I wanted to do two things: I wanted to be Superman first and foremost, but when I realized leaping tall buildings in a single bound was beyond me, my main dream became going to the NFL. Whether it is becoming a superhero, a doctor, a lawyer, or owning your own business, everyone at some point in time had the desire to be something great. What seems to happen is life hits us and we can no longer look towards tomorrow because we are so focused on the issues of today. James Dean said, "Dream as if you'll live forever and live as if you'll die today."

What childhood dreams did you set for yourself? Did those dreams continue to evolve throughout your teenage years? As an adult, do you still dream, or have you simply started to accept where you are as your permanent place? The dream of making it to the NFL never happened for me, but many of my dreams did come true. The reason the others came true is that I never stopped setting new goals. I never stopped reaching for the stars and I was willing to start dreaming again. I am asking that on this journey towards purpose and fulfillment, you start doing the same.

Growing up, I could often be found playing tag in my neighborhood. I was very good at it. This was my NFL prep time and where I perfected my jukes and stiff-arms. I was fast and agile, and I knew for a fact there were certain people I could catch, and they were the ones I went after first when the game started. The older guys in the neighborhood, they were a different story. I knew I couldn't catch them right away, so I didn't pursue them as much. Even though I knew the reward would be great, after failing to tag them before, I decided it would just take too much to catch them. Instead, I went after the kids that were closer to my age and speed.

Looking back at it now, I wonder, is this how people view their goals and aspirations for the future, and is this the mindset that prevents them from taking action? Are you telling yourself, I'd rather focus on the people and things that are closest to me so that I am not vulnerable? Are you telling yourself that it isn't worth trying to shoot for the stars because you've tried and failed before and now you fear failing again?

Thomas Edison said, "I have not failed. I've just found 10,000 ways that won't work."

It is more honorable to face the reflection of failure than the reflection of regret. Failure hurts only when the ego is involved. If we reject the ego, then failure can be viewed as the **First Attempt In Learning** and not as a fatal error. Failure teaches you what didn't work.

Failure tends to put such a sour taste in our mouths that even the memory of it is a deterrent from trying again. But it is important, for the sake of everything you desire that you stomach it despite that taste and that you try again. American novelist Truman Capote put it best when he said, "Failure is the condiment that gives success its flavor."

4

It's Go Time!

"Every battle is won before it is fought." –Sun Tzu

B EFORE ANYTHING CAN be accomplished, it must be first envisioned in the mind. Once the mind actualizes what the desire is, it is then, and only then, that the body can begin to perform that which the mind intended it to do. There might be a multitude of things that stand in the way of accomplishing the thing you desire, but it first begins with the mind.

Here's the bottom line up front: The goal is to get to the top. To fulfill your purpose.

Getting to the top means rising to the highest level possible, crushing every goal you set for yourself, and maintaining that level of success without sacrificing who you are to get there. It means not allowing yourself to remain stagnant or use the justification that you were dealt a bad hand in order to give yourself a free pass. We have all gone through trying times, and if you haven't, one day you will.

One of the greatest challenges we face when it comes to reaching our purpose is that we have made it okay to quit on ourselves. We comforted others who have failed and refuse to try again and we have created a safe haven for those who lack effort, drive, passion, and motivation. Well, that safe haven does not exist here. What does exist here is accountability. You will learn to be accountable for your actions, just as you will own what comes as a result of your lack of action. I went from being expelled from high school my senior year, running away from home and sleeping in a stranger's basement, to serving my country as a United States Marine. This change didn't happen because I wished upon a star. It happened because I made the conscious decision to take sole responsibility for my actions and their outcomes.

I knew things needed to change for me and the only way to make that change happen was to leave the situation I was in. I needed to separate myself from the things I was connected to that were holding me back. I knew leaving wouldn't be easy, but I also knew it was necessary.

Many of the things I went through would have broken most people for good, and admittedly, some of them did break me. But the difference is, I was not broken for long. I was knocked down many times. During those moments when I was down, there was always something telling me I not only should get back up, but I needed to get up. Les Brown said, "When life knocks you down, try to land on your back because if you can look up, you can get up. Let your reason get you back up." Well, my reason did get me back up, and my reason was my family, my dreams, and you.

My ascension to where I am today is a product of my faith in God, my uncommon work ethic, and the knowledge that I was destined to walk amongst giants.

My job as a Marine was to support and defend my country against all enemies foreign and domestic. I did that for many years and in the end, I stood proud knowing I did it well. Now that I am no longer in uniform, there is another enemy that I want to help everyone else defend, and that is whatever is holding you back from being who it is you want to be.

My method of delivering this message might seem uncommon, but I feel that you will be able to see yourself in my personal stories and that they will help you gain a new outlook on your life and the future you envision. In the end, whatever enemies you are facing, you can and will, through the insight and strength you gain, have the faith to go out and conquer them. This book is about elevation. There will be many barriers to break through along the way, but if you simply make the commitment and make small, simple contributions towards attaining your goal every day, you will find that the things which you've hoped for is firmly within your grasp.

My desire to see you win is as great as my desires for myself. You may not believe this, but it is true. I genuinely want you to succeed, but I cannot want you to win more than you do. This was something that I dealt with for many years as a leader of Marines. My peers and subordinates would come to me with their goals, and I would spend countless hours outlining a plan and doing weekly coaching calls, but in the end, some still would not make any progress. Why? Because something else (their appetites, distractions, other priorities, etc.) was always bigger than their goals.

Wanting to reach the next level is going to take work. It is going to require you to make a full commitment to making your goals bigger than your distractions. Your appetite for success and fulfillment has to be as strong as your desires to scroll through social media or watch your favorite show. It is going to take a grand effort, and I am willing to help you get there.

What I am offering you here, only if you really want change, are game-changing and life-altering messages that if you put them to use, will ignite an eternal fire inside you that no amount of past fear, doubt, and lack of faith can extinguish.

So, if your inspiration battery is dead and you want to jumpstart your life, this book is here to be the set of jumper cables you need. And if you are serious about growth, serious about change, and serious about elevation, then connect the mental cables because I'm charged and ready to go!

5

People Don't
Want Change

H OW NICE WOULD it be to have the ideal body without having to
exercise? To pass the test without having to study. To get the relationship to work without learning to manage conflict. To be able to reap the
rewards of hard work without having to do the work at all. That would be
nice, wouldn't it?

Temporarily, that is.

You get a different feeling when you have put your all into something
and then it works out for your good. When things are just given to you, rarely
do you learn to genuinely appreciate them. To be able to have the end result
is what everyone wants. We crave the lifestyle but won't do the work it takes
to get there. We want the benefits that come with change but aren't willing to
work for them. The benefits of change are enticing because you can imagine
what it would feel like.

The thought of actually doing the work is where the issues arise. One
thing that keeps people from being able to change are competing commitments. Oftentimes we find ourselves more committed to what others want for
us than what we want for ourselves. Other competing thoughts are internal:
people are torn between what they want in the long run and what they want
right now. Right now gives me immediate gratification. Right now means
I don't have to think about tomorrow. The habit of being able to "Amazon

Prime" everything in life has prevented us from having enough patience to start the process and to see it through to our end goal.

Change will require a transformation. You can't be the same person you were five years ago and think you will be able to take your same mentality into new rooms. It is about growth. Nothing in the world stays the same. Just as all living species have evolved to be able to survive, so must you. As you journey with me through this book, I want your mind to go beyond evolving to just survive. You are destined to thrive, and we are going to start that trek together.

It's time to commit

In 1519, a man by the name Hernán Cortés set the standard for commitment when he arrived to the New World with the intention of conquering the land he found. As a declaration of his commitment, he told all of his men to burn their ships. The burning of the ships was significant because this meant they were eliminating the option of not finishing what they started.

Their act sent a clear message that there was no turning back. In order to reach the level of abundance that is your birthright, you must be willing to make this same type of commitment. You must remind yourself that there is no other option for you. Some of you cannot afford to turn back because your effort or lack of effort will echo through your life and the lives of everyone depending on you.

Are you up for the challenge? If you are, then which ship is it that you need to burn? Is it doubt, fear, and procrastination? Is it lack of initiative, not trusting in your own ability, or complacency? Whatever it is, it's time to burn the ships. Write down the top three things you need to burn in order to show yourself there is no turning back.

1. _____

2. _____

3. _____

Now that you have identified some of the ships you have to burn, we can truly get to work. We will do this by making a proclamation.

I took an oath when I joined the Marines and it was an oath that I would have to renew each time I reenlisted. The purpose of this was to reaffirm my commitment to myself, to the nation and people I served, and to the Corps. Now it's your turn. Please raise your right hand and read the following aloud:

> *I know that the thing I have inside of me is something phenomenal. Because of this, I refuse to walk the paved roads of mediocrity. Instead, I choose to navigate the troubled and murky waters of adversity until the dream I see when I close my eyes becomes the reality I possess when I wake.*

I wrote the above passage shortly after I realized I was all in. I had just made the decision to retire from the Marine Corps and to walk away from a sure promotion to Sergeant Major. For those not familiar with the military rank structure, this is the highest enlisted rank for Marines. Many of my peers told me I was crazy. They told me I needed to stay and finish it out. What they did not understand was that their push to get me to stay was nowhere near as strong as the magnetic pull my goals had for me to leave. Jim Rohn once said, "that the more powerful the purpose, the more powerful the pull."

Many people questioned what I was going to do once I retired. My response was, "I am going to be great!" To reach the level of greatness I was speaking of meant leaving what I was familiar with. It meant walking away from the safe and comfortable route and daring to believe in myself. If my dreams were keeping me up at night, I thought, then why not wake up and chase them. I knew I had to set fire to two of the ships in my world, and those were comfort and security.

If you have made it this far in the book, chances are there is a personal level of greatness you are seeking. To get there, you will need to do more than just reading about it. This is just the first step. The next step that needs to happen is to make hard work and drive for success a part of your DNA. Once you've done this, it won't feel like a task or a chore. It will become a subconscious daily habit when you fully embrace it and dedicate yourself to it. Here is what you will gain if you apply the lessons and tools I am giving you:

- Clarity
- Higher level of self-awareness, self-worth, self-management
- Renewed sense of purpose
- Confidence
- Passion
- Will to succeed
- Discipline
- Initiative

6

Change

BEFORE YOU CAN have any of the qualities I mentioned before, you have to be willing to change. Change can be viewed in many ways. If you're starting the new job you've always wanted, then change is great. But when it involves changing the person in the mirror, it is rarely ever welcomed without reservation.

In the Marine Corps, roughly every three years we had to pack up and move to another place. Sometimes it was a few states away, and other times it meant moving to the other side of the world. Whether I wanted to move or not, I had to go.

Here's the thing: each time we got to the new place, we found ourselves deeply in love with the change. We may have been planted in one location, but growth happened each time we were uprooted.

When planting trees, all saplings start in a small container. As they grow, they must be repotted so that the roots can continue to spread and the trees can grow into what they are meant to become. Without adequate space, plants will never be able to grow to their max potential so a change in the environment is a must. Change is necessary if you ever want to be able to produce fruit. Producing the fruit will also require you to change. It might be a change in your physical location or moving to a new job. Just like a transplanted tree, a change of environment can spark new growth for you.

Being uprooted is never comfortable. However, you never know what experiences and growth are in store for you until you get there. Oftentimes the hardest change to make is the one that is needed most. The greatest challenge is changing your mindset. But if you're willing, it will ultimately lead you towards growth, purpose, and fulfillment.

As human beings, we tend to hesitate in doing the thing that is necessary while we are eager to do the things that are easy. Where has that brought us? Are we any further along in this journey because of those decisions or are we still in the same place?

I once read a quote that said, "The scariest place to be is in the same place as last year." Yet many of us find ourselves there year in and year out, largely due to our unwillingness to change. We fight against growth. Why is it that we oppose what is good for us? Why are we so reluctant to change? Is it out of fear of the unknown? Are we too afraid to step away from certainty?

It takes courage to do something different, but that fear should be enough to motivate you. We refuse to modify our behaviors, yet we expect the things we desire to fall into our laps by just thinking good thoughts, putting the idea out into the atmosphere, and expecting it to manifest. Well, that is a good start, but it also takes work. It takes you making a conscious effort to get started, and it all begins with altering the most complex organism in your body: your brain. We must work to rewire our thinking so that change can occur. For most people, it is easier to stay in the same place than to take the chance on doing something new.

Adam Grant, in his book *Think Again,* said that "we often prefer the ease of hanging on to old views rather than grappling with the difficulty of new ones." Change is a new idea that troubles us. We want to progress, but the mere thought of meeting adversity deters us. It makes us hesitant to act, resulting in a life that is stagnant and lacks fulfillment and purpose. To get to where you want to be, you are going to have to learn to change your attitudes, habits, and behaviors.

Everything we do starts in the mind. One of my favorite quotes is: "Thoughts become words, words become actions, actions become character, and character is everything." We will either poison our journey in its infancy stage with toxic thoughts or we will speak life into it.

Our attitudes are our settled ways of thinking about things. The results of our attitudes are shown in our behavior. Behavior is the way in which someone conducts themselves, specifically towards other people. What people make of our behavior becomes our character to them. The field of psychology takes it a step further and says, "Behavior is an action, activity, or process which can be observed and measured." The observation of behavior becomes evident in a person's regular tendencies or practices. It is especially prominent in tendencies that are hard to give up, which are called habits.

Habits are the things that we must change in order to elevate. Although there is adversity in change, there is also beauty. Nature has shown us this with the butterfly; there are many lessons that can be learned from the transformation of a butterfly. The caterpillar must go through not only a change but a metamorphosis to reach their full potential. From the time they are born, they eat continuously to provide their body with the nutrients needed to grow. When they are not eating, they are resting and hiding for survival. During this time, the caterpillar will shed its skin up to five times. Each time, the shedding is so they can continue to grow. The last shed before the major transformation happens when they become a chrysalis. This is the hard outer shell where they will rest and undergo the metamorphosis into a butterfly.

If you consider this process, you will notice that before change could occur, the caterpillar needed to feed itself. For us, this part of the process involves gaining knowledge. Elevation requires knowledge and knowledge comes through effort. It is impossible to elevate without building up the mind. An intelligent heart acquires knowledge, and the ear of the wise seeks knowledge (Proverbs 18:15).

The shedding of the skin represents the need to transform. Growth can only occur when you shed the former self. As the caterpillar hardened, you will need to as well. The reason for creating a hard shell is that as you walk along the road to greatness, you will be met with much adversity. You will need to have a hard outer layer or armor, figuratively speaking, in order to withstand the attacks that will surely come. Regardless of whether the attacks come from within yourself in the form of doubt or externally in the form of criticism, there is beauty when you persevere. There is beauty when you become what you have always desired to be and when you learn to walk in your purpose. Therefore, whether you want to change or not, your success is dependent upon you gaining knowledge and being willing to transform.

When I was a kid, I went on a field trip to a small farm. While there, I had the opportunity to see what it was like to use farm tools, feed live animals, and how they went about producing things for the market. One thing that stood out to me the most was watching someone take a lump of clay and turn it into something of greater value. To see something go from an idea to creation. To watch the shape change over and over until their vision became reality. Over the years, I never forgot about that potter's wheel and I have always imagined our lives as that lump of clay.

From that day forward, I knew whatever I wanted to do, I could. There is no such thing as wrong when you are the artist. When you are creating your own masterpiece, your vision is what is right.

Change means getting on the potter's wheel to reshape and mold yourself again. The reshaping process is going to hurt for a few reasons. It is going to force you to face the person in the mirror and do a real self-assessment, but once you've done that, you will be in a position where transforming is inevitable. On the journey of change, you will notice some things you thought were good for you, but, in reality, have been stifling your progression. Let's start there.

Reshaping and molding will force you to dig up some things you tried to bury long ago. Things like shame, guilt, and past failures. Things like broken family relationships or the apology and closure you desperately needed but never received. Regardless, it is time to get back on the wheel to recast those things that serve only to weigh you down. You do not need to carry their weight any longer. That apology may never come no matter how much you want it to. Dwelling on the negative event only hurts your mental health and prevents you from being completely free. It is an anchor that you no longer need—remember, you've already burned your ships.

Your work of reshaping at the potter's wheel is going to be more than getting rid of the external factors. That's the easy part in the grand scheme of things. The hardest part in this endeavor is going to be tackling the root because oftentimes the root….is you.

Some of the most beautiful pieces of art in this world started on the potter's wheel and you are no different. You'll make mistakes in the process and you may need to start all over again, but if you remain moldable and willing to change, the results of your nascent ideas, once fully transformed, will be greater than you could have ever imagined. It is the willingness to be shaped that will prepare the way for true growth. Every experience, be it good or bad, plays a vital role in shaping us into who we are today, and the actions you take or refuse to take will shape you into the person you'll become tomorrow.

The thing I realize about the clay of life is that the clay itself had no say in being on the wheel. You, on the other hand, do. Your willingness to get on the wheel will determine how your habits, behaviors, and attitude will change.

Our minds have been shaped by internal and external influences. Not all the hands that have shaped us have had our best interests at heart. There have also been people in your life who have prevented you from getting to your purpose. Knowing this, you must answer this question.

What does your inner circle look like?

If we really are the average of the five people we spend the most time with, we need to pause and reevaluate our circle. I'm sure you've heard the saying before, but don't just read that and let it be another line in a book that you will soon forget.

Take a second and think of who you spend the most time with and ask yourself another hard question: Are they adding value to you or are you adding value to them? One of you is on the potter's wheel at any given moment. Who has been influencing whom the most?

7

The Butterfly

THERE IS A story of a little boy who was playing in a park with a few of his friends. While attempting to catch the ball from one of his buddies, he came up short and the ball rolled under a nearby bush. While retrieving the ball, he became distracted by butterflies making their way out of their chrysalises. Fascinated with the butterflies, he tossed the ball back to his friends and crouched down by the bush to observe. He was amazed as he watched the colors begin to show.

The little boy saw that the process was taking a while and decided to open the chrysalis a little to help one of the butterflies out. He opened it and the butterfly fell to the ground, flapped its wings for a while, but soon died. The boy looked at the butterfly and said to himself, "Maybe I didn't get to it fast enough." He quickly moves over to the other chrysalises and starts to open them up. Some of the butterflies were further along than the others and soon took off in flight, but most of them fell to the ground around him and died.

The boy ran home feeling heartbroken over the butterflies. His mother saw him and asked, "What's wrong?"

Emphatically, the boy said, "I was trying to save the butterflies that were trapped in those bags, Mom, but I couldn't."

She said to him, "What bag, son?"

He said, "Mom the butterflies were stuck and trying to get out of these bags in the bush and they couldn't no matter what I did. I tried helping them but I just couldn't."

Finally, after giving it thought the mother realized what the boy was trying to tell her. She said "Son, wait a second. That bag you're speaking of is called a chrysalis and I need you to understand something about that. When this process begins, it is nature's sign that the transformation from caterpillar to a butterfly is complete and the butterfly is ready to leave the chrysalis. When you opened the chrysalis, you interfered in a key part of the life cycle for the butterfly. You see, son, the butterfly has to go through this struggle. It looks hard for a reason. As the butterfly struggles, its heart rate elevates and the fluid in the center of the body begins to travel out to the wings, making them open. I know you were trying to help, but by removing the butterfly from that struggle, you prevented it from being able to fly."

Why do I tell you this story of the butterfly and the little boy? In life, you will go through many struggles. Many of those struggles you will be able to handle, but there will be many others that you will want someone to remove you from. These are struggles that you must go through so that you develop the skills needed to fly. Struggle is a transformation we must endure to be able to reach our full potential. When we learned to walk, we only found our balance point by falling many times. On the journey towards purpose and fulfillment, learning to embrace the struggle is part of the process. You can't know joy without experiencing pain and you can't appreciate the freedom of flight without experiencing the struggle.

8

Growth

IN 2012, I did my first of many bodybuilding and men's physique competitions. It was a local show held on base in Okinawa, Japan, for the servicemembers and local Japanese citizens. Preparing for a bodybuilding show without a coach took a lot of research and required me to have even more discipline than competitors who did have the guidance of a coach. Since I didn't know what to do, I went online and found what I thought was the best method. The result of those twelve weeks of boiled chicken, brown rice, and asparagus was a third-place trophy. Being the competitor I am, third place wasn't good enough. I decided I wanted to do another show but wanted to take some time to build quality muscle, so that meant switching from competition prep mode to full off-season mode. The plan was always to come back a little bit bigger and a little bit better than before. This meant it was time to grow and growth happened in a few ways. The intensity of the training sessions increased, the amount of food I ate went up, and I started training to hit muscle failure. Because of the progressive muscle overload, the muscles began to adapt and subsequently grew. I would go on to win multiple shows but the successes I had competing really aren't the point of the story.

The point of the story is that there were necessary steps to growth that I had to follow if I wanted to accomplish my goal. The first thing I did was identify a goal I wanted to accomplish. Then, I made a plan and put the plan into action. No matter how good that plan is, there will always be something that could potentially go wrong. You might not hit every mark. You may fail at times, but if you never give up on yourself, you can see it through.

1. *Write down five things you want to accomplish.*

2. *Write down five things that could potentially stand in the way of you accomplishing them.*

3. *Write down what's at stake if you don't accomplish your goal(s).*

9

Motivation is Temporary,
Discipline is the Key

I F YOU DO not possess the knowledge, skills, drive, and initiative to keep it in motion, you will never develop what is needed to succeed. Many people get caught in the vicious cycle of reading motivational quotes, listening to motivational speakers, and thinking that the spark of motivation it ignites is going to carry them all the way through the finish line. The truth is that it won't. In order to be fulfilled, you must take action.

You are truly motivated and driven by purpose when you have identified the destination you want to get to, the things you want to do when you get there, and in the back of your mind, the people who desperately need you to get there most. This is what causes your motivation to spread like wildfire. False motivation is like an ember in the storm, easily extinguished at the first drop of rain. False motivation can only get you so far. You can only hide behind the mask of intensity, passion, and being a "go-getter" for so long before you are exposed. Real motivation ignites an internal fire that burns bright. Real motivation continues to burn until it consumes everything around it. When all you can think about is accomplishing that goal. When all you dream about is becoming who you want to be. It is listening to that motivational speech, creating action steps, and putting in the work afterward. Creating a list of steps helps you become more consistent, and consistency coupled with discipline are the things you need to take you to the next level. The work that you put in every day is what ultimately leads to transformation.

The self-determination theory (SDT) says that motivation comes from both intrinsic and extrinsic factors. Both types of forces shape who we are and how we behave. SDT is about being able to make your own decisions and not allowing anyone else to determine things for you. You must be in control of your own destiny.

Many of us have things we say we want to do. Many of us feel we have been called to a specific purpose, yet we haven't started on the path of fulfilling what it is we are purposed to do. Others have started and have since then stopped. If this is you, maybe you stopped because you got tired. You stopped because you didn't reach success as quickly as you thought you would and you gave in to disappointment. You gave up in a situation where you were building up momentum but then mental fatigue hit and you decided you no longer wanted to continue because you couldn't see the finish line.

How many times have you started on the quest to fulfilling a desire only to stop short of accomplishing whatever it was? Why do we do that to ourselves? Do you not deserve to have the feeling of accomplishing your deepest desires? Do you not think you have the capacity? Yes, you do. You have the ability to do it, but you also have that little thing called doubt knocking at your door, preventing you from jumping back into the fight and finishing it. Letting doubt creep in is the fastest way to watch your dreams get knocked out. To prevent this from happening, it's time to put a guard up around your vision.

Your fight is to create for the next generation. Your fight is to create for those that look up to you. Your job is to create for the creator who created you with a thought in mind that you would come into this world and that you would seek to be fulfilled and live out your true divine purpose. That you will live out whatever it is you desire to maximize your potential as a human being. In order to do that, you are going to have to be able to get through every round of your fight.

Many of your goals lie waiting for you. You can't burn out in the first mile of this marathon. Speed kills. Slow and steady will be what it takes to win this race. The race does not belong to the swift, but to the one who endures to the end. You must be willing to see it through.

You have to understand that there's a difference between being motivated and having discipline. There's a difference between saying you are going to do something and doing it until it's done. By saying you're going to do something and then making an excuse for why it didn't happen, you are only prolonging the journey to get to where you ought to be. I don't have a safe place for people who say, "It's too hard for me," or "I don't think I can do it anymore," or "It's not for me anymore." The first question I would have is: Why? Why is it that you feel what you wanted to do for so long is no longer for you? Now, if you can give me a good reason that is solely based on you and what you desire and that truly explains why you stopped chasing certain things, then I can understand. That wouldn't be considered quitting; that's a pivot. Sometimes you need to pivot away from a situation if you realize it's a dead end, but you can't just quit because it's not working out right now.

The reason many people don't see it through is because they are missing a key component in the success equation. You must be disciplined. The word discipline itself is derived from the Latin word *discipulus,* which means to learn. You must become a disciple of your own craft and you must study it and work to perfect it. In the pursuit of change, you must learn how to do things in a different way. You have to look at the totality of your efforts over time and learn what works for you. During this process of becoming disciplined, you will learn where you are strong and where you are weak. You will learn what your level of patience is and where your personal breaking point is. When you get to that breaking point, that's when challenges arise and people walk away, but in finding that breaking point, if you stay on the gas, you find discipline.

Having the discipline to keep strong in one's efforts despite not seeing the finish line is what creates real consistency.

Consistency is broken when you get to the crossroads of difficulty and challenge and you make the decision to sleep in. It is broken when you decide that it isn't worth studying one more time.

In sports, the greatest athletes become great because they are consistent in their approach to practicing their craft. Even though they have shot thousands of free throws, some of the best basketball players have been known to go to the gym before practice and work more on their free throws, go to practice, and when practice is over, practice their free throws again. Even though they are fully confident in their abilities, their desire is to be disciplined with everything they do and consistent with every movement so that when the day comes and their skills are put to the test, they are prepared to win the game.

Are you working towards your goals this way? Are you doing more than what it takes or are you doing just enough to satisfy yourself? Free throws are the simplest things to do yet many people don't put forth the effort to practice because it isn't as sexy as driving to the hoop and doing a lay-up. But here's the thing: many games are won and lost by free throws. It is the small things that end up winning the game for us or costing us the title in the long run. Whether you are being challenged in the office, in your home, or in your mind, it's time to start focusing on free throws again. We must put time into the simplest things if we are going to be able to elevate.

Through your discipline, your character is shown. In the Marine Corps Martial Arts Program, also known as MCMAP, we would teach service members about three important areas of discipline: physical, mental, and character. The combination of these three qualities were known as the synergies of the system. The goal is to develop a balance of all of these in order to be as effective as possible both in the office and on the battlefield. The problem arises when there isn't an effective balance.

To get to where you want to be, you will need to develop the same three disciplines and these tools will help you along the way.

Mental Discipline

1. **Identify your distractions.**

   Many people will not reach greatness because they cannot separate themselves from their distractions. When you identify your distractions, you identify the root cause of your inaction. A distraction is anything that takes your attention away from your desired area of focus. They prevent you from staying on course and they keep you mentally occupied. They are the things that prevent someone from giving full attention to something else. Your intention needs to be greater than what's vying for your attention. The light of the distraction can't be brighter than the light of your goals.

For some of you, your distractions are the company you keep. If you are surrounding yourself with people who lack focus, there can only be one outcome from your interactions. Distracted people can only do one thing and that's distract you. The reason for this is that they don't have a focus. How can they appreciate what you're doing and not distract you if they've never had a vision like you do?

Recognize your personal distractions and get rid of them.

2. **Plan for your success.**

The greatest leaders, entrepreneurs, and business professionals are the best planners. Planning is the planting of mental seeds for tomorrow, and the daily execution of your plans serve as the watering. Repeating the planning process daily will eventually lead to a harvest. It is amazing what you can accomplish when your actions and efforts match your original intentions. Planning closes that gap.

Plan like your future depends on it. Because it does.

3. **Find a Mentor.**

You can't go at it alone. Having a mentor who is experienced in the space you're trying to get into, who is someone you value, and is someone who can give sound advice is a great start to developing mental discipline. You need a mentor because the great ones have the ability to look at your life and your situation and steer you along the right course.

Your mentor should believe in you and your destination.

Physical Discipline

1. **Make time for yourself.**

   You only have one body and you must take care of it. It doesn't matter what you want to accomplish in life, if you don't take care of the one vessel that gives you the ability to do so, you'll never accomplish what you desire. Taking care of your physical body also serves to put mental rejuvenation into your schedule. There are countless benefits to physical activity. It is vitally important for all facets of health, mental and physical, to make time for yourself. Aim for at least 30 minutes of physical activity at least three days a week. Taking your body through something physical can lead to an improved mood, clearer thinking, and better performance. Your health is your wealth.

2. **Go beyond comfort.**

   Your workout routine can eventually become just that—a routine. As humans, our bodies adapt easily to what we ask of it. Breaking that routine means stepping out and pushing yourself in a new way. If traditional yoga is your thing and you're good at it, try hot yoga. If you're into long distance running, consider interval training with anaerobic activities like push-ups, leg lifts, and squats to add complexity.

3. **Set attainable goals.**

   Too often when people start a physical training regime, the goal is to lose weight, gain muscle, or perform a task better. The problem is rarely ever the goal, it's typically the timeline associated with it. Wanting to get to the finish line too soon can lead to an early physical burnout if you aren't careful. The answer to this problem is to set attainable goals and continue moving the needle as you reach them.

Character Discipline

1. **Develop your character.**

   What will others say to your actions? What will they speak of your deeds? Character development is tied to your morals and values. It is about what you honor. It is how you carry yourself. And, more often than not, your character will enter a room long before you do and stay long after you leave, so being a person of good character goes a long way.

2. **Know your worth.**

   When you know your worth, you are less likely to entertain something that is below you. When you are unsure of your worth or you let someone else define it for you, your character takes the hit because you begin acting in a way that isn't indicative of who you truly are and what your value is.

3. **Visit your values.**

   Visiting your values means taking a look at where you are and what you're doing and asking yourself the hard question, "Am I living according to my values?" If you aren't, then revisiting them means writing out what means the most to you and doing what needs to be done to change your actions to align with those values you've identified. If what you're doing isn't in line with your values, then you're at a risky imbalance and this leads to character flaws.

10

Keys and Locks

THERE WAS A janitor who had just started working at the local college. When he got there, the previous guy just handed him the keys and told him he was quitting that day. Now, I'm sure we all remember what a set of janitor keys looked like—there are a lot. There were short keys, long keys, and keys that were color coded. There were also keys that were rusted and looked like they hadn't opened anything in years.

Within the first few days on the job, the new janitor found himself flustered every day as he tried to make sense of all the keys. Teachers would come to him when they were locked out, and this rattled him because it would take him at least five minutes just to figure out which key went to their room. Weeks went by and he would constantly say to himself that he was never going to figure out which keys fit which locks. One Saturday he woke up and said he was going to go in and he would unlock every door in that school so he could finally know which key corresponded to which lock. And so he did.

He showed up before the sun rose and opened the front door of the school. Starting with the main office, he opened the door for the principal and every office clerk. Then he went to the registrar's office and to every classroom. All the extra keys that didn't work he discarded. By the end of the day, he had successfully matched every key to its lock.

I share this story with you because life is also about keys and locks. You will come upon many locked doors and it will be your job to figure out which key unlocks them. Where persistence and patience may be the key that unlocks one door, emotion regulation and a calm demeanor may be the key to another. With your family or coworkers, you will need to figure out which teaching key or leadership tool unlocks each relationship. The goal of unlocking these relationships is so that people can become receptive to what you have to give. Just as that janitor grew frustrated in the beginning because he couldn't find the key to a door he needed to open, you too will have those challenging moments trying to figure out how to unlock certain things in your life. But once you figure out what key opens a particular door for you, you must mark it.

Be aware of the doors you will run into. There are doors you are meant to go through and others you must stay away from. And for each door you decide to enter, there are things that need to be done before you can get in.

- **Trap doors** — These doors are a representation of anything that stops you from being great and reaching your vision. They are designed to keep you in place so stay vigilant.

- **Revolving doors** — These are the doors that you may have to go in and out of, but be careful not to get caught up. You need to know how to properly time your entrance and exit.

- **False doors** — These are the doors that serve to distract you and lead you off course. Don't spend time trying to unlock them. There's nothing there for you.

- **Glass doors** — These are meant for you to be able to see through to identify if what's behind them is what you truly want. It can be a motivator or a deterrent. It depends on where your heart is and what your desires are.

11

Increasing the Demand

IN 2018, ELON Musk and his company, Tesla, had a lot threatening their success. They had experienced many failures. There were lawsuits, recalls, and to make matters worse, his company fell victim to a cyberattack. What he did during this time was something that most wouldn't do during a crisis. Instead of folding under the pressure, he fully committed himself to getting his company to the level it needed to be. He vowed to position himself "wherever there was a problem in Tesla." To those on the outside, his commitment looked like unhealthy obsession. It wasn't a rare thing to see him sleeping on the factory floor. He didn't do that because there were high demands for his cars, he did it because of the increased demands on himself. When asked why he was sleeping on the floor, his response was, "Because I don't have time to go home and shower." A little over three years later, those efforts would earn him a net worth of 292 billion dollars, making him the richest man on earth.

As the owner of Tesla, Musk knew that he had a responsibility to take care of his team, to correct the company's deficiencies, and accomplish their overall mission. He knew that only *he* would be held accountable for what came from not doing it. He saw the need and in response, demanded more from himself. Did he really have to sleep on the floor to get to this end result? Probably not. Did he go all in? Absolutely. By no means am I telling you that you need to stay at the office and not go home. That isn't the healthiest of habits, but what I am saying is that you need to find that same level of commitment for your personal growth if you truly want your dream to become a reality. Start demanding more from yourself.

When a company has a superior product, public demand for it increases. Now the company must grow in order to meet the new demand. You too have a supply, but that supply is stored up for the future you, and it is time to start increasing the demands on yourself to create it. Increasing your personal demands is a critical part of reaching success.

So what happens when you demand more of yourself? When there is an increase in demand, the result is an increase in the price and quantity of a good.

Here is what this looks like if we apply this to ourselves. You begin to increase the demands on yourself to be more productive. To meet those demands, you must increase your daily output. What that looks like is waking up earlier, not accepting partial products from yourself, and making sacrifices today so that you can have what you want tomorrow.

There are some of us who have what it takes to do this and others who won't be up to the challenge. You can be one of the few who do if you put forth the effort. Elon Musk doesn't have to be an anomaly. You can add yourself to that number. There is more than enough room at the top for you and anyone else who is willing to face the mirror, speak power into their promise and their purpose, and act on it.

Admiral Chester Nimitz stated that during the battle of Iwo Jima, "uncommon valor was a common virtue." Acts of bravery that were rarely seen on the battlefield were commonplace during that time, because there were no other options. The servicemembers could either die running away from the gunfire or they could stand up to the formidable enemy and take the fight to their doorstep. That's exactly what they did, and it is precisely what you must do. You must take the fight to the doorstep of mediocrity. You must take the fight directly to vanquish procrastination. You must kick down the door of uncertainty, demand more of yourself, and fight with everything you have to get to what belongs to you.

Life has happened to you and life is going to continue to happen to you. There is nothing you can do about that. There's no way you can prevent it. What you can do is change the verbiage and say that the events happened *for* you.

There are four seasons and each of those seasons bring about different things. Just as the seasons change, so will you. Every day cannot be great. There has to be balance in the world and you must accept that. You will have up days and down days. You will have days when it seems like everything is going in your favor and then there will be other days that make you ask, "Am I losing my mind?" What has happened to you in the past does matter but what matters most is how you react to it. You must increase the demands despite the situation, despite the lack of resources, and without adequate support. You are going to have to start changing the language you use in adverse situations. If you had something happen to you, recognize it for what it is, then change the language. It is okay to ask, "Why did this happen to me?" It is not okay to allow it to control you.

Think about a time when things didn't pan out as you'd hoped. What was it that affected you the most? Why did it affect you? Answer: It affected you because you cared. It is acceptable to try to figure out what the purpose was behind some moment of misfortune, but I will tell you this: the answer to why it all happened won't come to you while you're sitting around not executing. The answers will only come after the work has been done. Now that you have that understanding, it is time to live up to the standard you set with those demands and hold to the new standard of excellence you are worthy of.

Again, I'd like to reiterate that only you can define what success is to you. Therefore, you need to understand that you can't look at the demands that others have put on themselves and think that's the fail-proof method for getting where you want to be. Those demands worked for them; what will work for you and your goals could be entirely different. What you can look at are the steps they took to get there.

1. **Educate yourself**

   Seek knowledge in every way possible. The more knowledgeable you become in an area, the more confident you will be. You also gain some important things by educating yourself. With knowledge comes confidence and, most importantly, competence.

2. **Identify your pain points**

What problems are you dealing with and how can you solve them? What keeps you up at night and why? Make a note of these things and create action steps to address them. Remember to attack it one step at a time. When you uncover your pain points, there is the natural tendency to want to fix everything right away. By attempting to right every wrong all at once, you're only going to overwhelm yourself, which contradicts everything we are working towards. One pain point at a time.

3. **Push past discomfort**

When you get tired, frustrated, and feel like you want to quit, don't. You never know if your breakthrough is just ahead. Anything worth having is worth fighting for. And you never know, someone else may be watching you, looking to you as their North Star, and they need you to stay in the fight.

4. **Know when to pull back**

It is okay to reset. It is not okay to quit. There is a difference. There are several reasons why you might need a reset. Life will throw many things at you and oftentimes they can come in waves, giving you no time to regain your footing before the next one hits. This is not giving up or giving in. This is recognizing the need for self-care and managing that need effectively.

12

Failure

I HAVE HAD THE unique privilege to work side by side with some of the most talented, driven, hungry, and tenacious people in the world. These people were known as the go-getters, the motivators, the fire-and-forget weapon systems that got the job done even if they failed to make it happen on their first attempt. In the same breath, I'll tell you that there were a large number of others that served with me who had the potential to operate at that same higher level, yet failed to fully make the transition that would have changed their life's trajectory forever. So what was the difference?

The difference lies in what each of them did after coming up short. Every one of those people started in the same origin point in the profession we were in. Every one of them went to boot camp. Each of them got the same mental, physical, and emotional test for thirteen weeks to become Marines. All went to school for their jobs and were given the same set of annual requirements they needed to meet. The difference between the group that excelled and those who didn't is that, over time, failing or coming up short became a motivation for greatness for the former while it became a deterrent and an inhibitor to performance for the latter. Likewise, there are millions of people all over the world who have potential yet have not been able to bridge the gap between desire and attaining whatever that desire is.

One of the many reasons people do not close that gap is that they are just too afraid to fail. Many times they fear failure not because of how it will make them feel, but because they fear what everyone else will think, say, or do about it. How is it that we care so much about what others think about us and what we do, when much of the time, those people we are so preoccupied with don't think about us at all? Stop giving others the power over your mind. If it's not others' ridicule that you fear, then you need to move past whatever is causing you to miss the mark. It is time to shoot your shot without thinking about anyone but yourself and those who truly support you. You might be aiming for the bullseye but for now, I just need you to get on the target. We can make small adjustments as we go.

One of the most important steps is knowing that failing doesn't make you a failure. It doesn't mean it's over, and it doesn't mean you can't try again. As you mature, you will grow to appreciate the lessons that comes with failure. Many times, failure will be essential. In order to succeed, you're going to have to stop seeing failure as the end, because it isn't. It is an opportunity for you to look at what you're trying to do from a different perspective and continue to refine your approach toward accomplishing that mission.

Our world is full of testimonies that show that persevering after failing produces quality outcomes. When the pressure on you increases, or when a wrench is thrown in your plan, if you're able to improvise and adapt, you will overcome and you will grow. One thing I learned in this thing called life is that failure is inevitable, but so is success if you keep trying!

On the path towards success, there are going to be many failures. There will be many setbacks. As beautiful as this life may be, there are going to be many times when it will knock you on your butt. The real test of character comes after that. Albert Einstein once said, "I have tried ninety-nine times and have failed, but on the hundredth time came success." Do you have what it takes to get back up and continue on after you fall or fail? Can you and are you willing to weather that storm? Can you withstand blow after blow and keep moving forward?

Boxers know best

Boxing is one of the greatest metaphors for life. One of the greatest fights I have ever watched was Tyson Fury vs. Deontay Wilder. This fight was the true definition of perseverance, dedication, discipline, pride, willpower, strength, and fortitude. Deontay Wilder is known as one of the most powerful punchers in the sport. When he hits someone with a clean shot, they go down and they go down hard. It is rare that a person recovers after Wilder's punches connect. One shot from "the Bronze Bomber" and they are out for the count.

His opponent, Tyson Fury, had been away from the boxing world for a while. After having immense success, he began to spiral downhill fast. The life of drugs, fast cars, and money started taking a toll on the former champion. He was no longer in contest shape ready to fight for world titles. Instead, he had been fighting off weight gain at over 400 pounds, struggling with drug addiction, and battling depression. This was all soon to change. With news that a potential fight for the title with Wilder was possible, he decided to clean things up and make another run at the title. He took his training to another level. He knew if he was going to fight someone of this caliber, everything he was doing needed to change. He would have to face off with his own failures before he could ever enter the ring again.

By the time fight day came, he weighed 256.5 pounds and was ready to conquer the world. When the fight began, it was everything boxing fans wanted to see. Finally someone was able to challenge the champ and make him work until—BOOM! With 2 minutes and 21 seconds left on the clock in the 12th round, Deontay Wilder connects with the shot everyone expected him to land. A vicious right hand followed by a powerful left hook sends his opponent to the canvas. But the difference this time is that his opponent was Tyson Fury, a man on a different level. Staring at the ceiling, Fury can hear the referee beginning to count. On the other side of the ring, Deontay Wilder is dancing with a look of victory on his face as if the fight was already over, but when the referee got to six, Tyson Fury looked at him and rose to his feet. He would go on to finish the round and the fight ended in a draw.

After being out of boxing for so long, how was Tyson Fury able to get back up? Where did he get the power to come back after suffering a blow like that? After taking all of those shots, I pictured him in that moment hearing the referee count and saying to himself, "You gotta get up. You gotta get up, you worked too hard for this. You have to believe in yourself. They are doubting you. Think about your wife, think about your kids, think about everybody who believes in you. Think about the ridicule you'll face if you don't get up. Think about how many people are gonna laugh at you. Think about how many people are gonna say, 'I told you he couldn't do it.' Think about how you were on drugs, how you were intoxicated and ready to commit suicide. Get up because failure is not an option. Finish this fight!" This fight was the true definition of perseverance, of dedication, of discipline, of pride, of willpower, of strength, and of fortitude.

In their rematch, Tyson Fury showed exactly who he is. He showed what resilience is. He showed what the will to succeed is. He showed that when you embrace the pain, when you embrace the training, when you embrace all the negatives that come along with getting to the level of success that you desire, it is all worth it in the end. He would go on to definitively beat the Bronze Bomber in their next engagement. None of this would have been possible if he hadn't done the work before the fight. We are talking about someone who at one point wanted to end his life. Someone who had tasted success in the past yet still found himself dealing with some real issues. This goes to show that you can fail but you can also fail forward.

Failure can derail any train but if you believe in yourself enough and you address the things that are hindering your progress, you will be able to get back on track. When life starts throwing the heavy punches and it seems like failure is inevitable, know that you may get knocked down, but you can get up before you're counted out.

Are you willing to get back up? I challenge you to reach deep within yourself and harness the willpower needed to get back up and win your fight!

13

The Deadly Cs

T HE WATERS OF the deadly Cs have captured many lives and there will
be countless more that follow. It is a slow death. One that you don't see
or feel until you are drowning in its depths.

These waters seem to pose no threat. There are no ripples and there
are no waves. There is no uncertainty and there is nothing lurking beneath.
This is precisely why people choose to stay and not venture out into the deep.

You see, in the deep, that is where there is trouble. That is where you
will have to prove that you can navigate your way out of it. That is where you
will face possible shipwreck and have to learn to swim, tread water, and hold
your breath. That is where your life skills will be put to test and where your
level of resilience will carry you or fail you…but the deep won't kill you. The
deep is where you will grow and develop the skills needed to conquer the
deadly Cs. What are those?

Comfort and Complacency.

Dictionary.com defines comfort as "a state of physical ease and freedom from pain or constraint" and defines complacency as "a feeling of quiet
pleasure or security, often while unaware of some potential danger, defect,
or the like; self-satisfaction or smug satisfaction with an existing situation,
condition, etc."

Learning to navigate the waters of comfort and complacency isn't easy.
It is for this reason so many people would rather stay in the comfortable

shallows. In order to conquer the Cs, you're going to have to place yourself in positions outside of what you're good at. You are going to need to go where you are vulnerable. You will need to take chances. Nothing has ever been conquered without a fight and without breaking habits of laziness, lack of initiative, and comfort. Whatever you wish to accomplish, it is going to take you fighting for it to achieve it. How will you be able to conquer comfort and complacency? It starts with making a commitment.

Make a commitment

Being committed is about doing what you said you would do. When you are committed to something, you are restricted from the freedoms you had before because you are now obligated to the task you agreed to. Signing a lease binds you to an apartment for the timeline specified within the contract. For those six months to a year, you are dedicated to the cause of taking care of the property, keeping everything in good order, and paying the rent on time. This is not just because the contract binds you to it. It is bigger than that. It is about doing it because you said you would.

Most people would never break a contract with someone else, but it is so easy to break a contract with ourselves. We are willing to quit on ourselves before we let someone else down. We are willing to commit to someone else's idea or someone else's agenda, but when it comes to us and doing what we need to do, somehow commitment becomes difficult. It becomes difficult because we give ourselves free passes after free passes. We tell ourselves it's okay that you skipped the gym today. It's okay that you turned in the homework assignment a little late—at least you turned it in. Well, it's not okay. It is unacceptable for you to make a commitment to yourself and to not make yourself and your goals a priority. Commitments require you to back up what you say with action.

Talk is cheap!

At least that's what they say. I personally do not agree with that. I think talking alone is expensive. I think saying you are going to do something and not following through comes at a cost that not many people are fully able to understand. Talk is not cheap.

Talking alone can cost your relationships. When you got married you made a vow and openly stated the things you would do to ensure the relationship would flourish. If you said you would do things that never got done, those things are not just forgotten. You made a solemn promise and either you stayed true to it or you didn't. Although relationships at home, at work, among friends aren't about keeping score (at least they shouldn't be), the understanding that you are not willing to follow through with a commitment says, "Find someone else to do it." It says, "Maybe I will, maybe I won't." It says that you're comfortable and complacent.

Talking alone can cause you to lose a position you were given. Your ability to talk got you there, but your inability to finish what you said you would do puts you at risk of having everything taken away. So no, talk is not cheap. It is very expensive.

Talk costs you your goals.

Was the night out on the town that important? Did you need to buy that round for your friends? When you got that test score back, was the party you went to instead of studying worth it? We are so easily thrown off course when we start choosing "right now" over what is right. When we allow our wants to override our needs.

Talking makes us feel good. Nowadays, it is all about "putting it in the atmosphere." Speaking things into existence. That's all good, and I encourage positivity, but when there is no progress to support what you say, you will find yourselves stuck in the same position you were in before. Talking with no action. If you want to start a business, start it. Do it the right way. Reach out to someone who has experience in the field you want to work in. Do research on the market in your area to see if your business idea would be suitable there.

Be smart about it. Don't try to open a pizza spot right next to Dominos. Get assistance with a business plan and allow those with the expertise to help identify any unforeseen pitfalls you may run into. This is how you go from talking about something to putting it into action.

Kobe Bryant is considered to be one of the greatest basketball players of all time. Some would argue he was the best, and it would be hard to refute that claim. He was a master of conquering comfort and complacency. The Black Mamba, as he was called, was ferocious on the basketball court. He could drive, he could shoot, he could play defense, and he was a great trash talker. The difference between Kobe and the other players who trash talked was that he was able to back it up. And not just because he was a great basketball player. He was able to back it up because of his competence and his confidence in his abilities for the game. His mindset, the Mamba mentality, was developed over time. Kobe was known for being the first in the gym and the last to leave. He refused to be outworked. He refused to willingly give another team the upper hand. Not only was he competitive during games, but his will to win even challenged his closest teammates to move up or move out of the way. Kobe's commitment to himself and his teammates is why he became one of the greatest that ever played the game.

By making a commitment and sticking to it, you separate yourselves from those who just talk. Burning your ships and not taking any action after that is pointless. If you made the decision to not turn back, you should have a plan of attack and be willing to work towards mission accomplishment. Being stranded with no plan leaves you vulnerable to accepting other options because you failed to take the appropriate steps. It shows that you are comfortable and complacent.

During the peak of Operations Iraqi Freedom and Enduring Freedom, servicemembers would go on patrols for numerous reasons: to gather intelligence, a show of force, and area reconnaissance to name a few. After months of doing the same thing, patrolling down the same roads, checking vehicles at the same checkpoint, it could have been easy to see it as just another day. Some might have been tempted to take a much-needed rest and believed it to be acceptable. Not for those on the ground it wasn't. For two Marines, Corporal Jonathan Yale and Lance Corporal Jordan Haerter, complacency never set in. On April 22, 2008, in Ramadi, Iraq, they were on post together when a truck loaded with explosives came speeding towards their checkpoint. On the other side of the checkpoint were numerous Marines, civilians, and other servicemembers. As the truck came speeding through, the vigilant Marines opened fire on the vehicle, killing the assailants moments before the vehicle detonated, taking both of their lives. Had these two been complacent, had they not been focused on the task at hand, many other lives would have been lost that day. Because of their courage, dedication, and vigilance, they saved the lives of many others. They represented their nation honorably and will be remembered for the heroes they are. For their actions, they were both posthumously awarded Navy Crosses, the nation's second-highest honor for combat efforts.

The potential dangers of being complacent in life is never reaching the levels you could have. Complacency gives the false sense of security, like nothing bad can happen. To conquer complacency means realizing that the safety and security actually blinds you from the potential downfalls that lie ahead. The coronavirus pandemic of 2020 exposed many businesses that were complacent and also highlighted those who were agile and able to pivot to other operating models. Complacency causes you to become so comfortable that you stop looking for potential hazards. It is the quiet pleasure of mediocrity. The satisfaction of "this is enough" and "there is no need to do more." To conquer complacency, things need to be shaken up a bit. This can happen voluntarily, or, because life is funny like that, it can happen without you seeking change. For you as an individual, conquering complacency will allow you to do all that you desire with clear intention and focused efforts. It all starts with one of the most valuable steps, which is developing new habits.

Out with the old, in with the new

There are not many better ways to change behavior than with repetition. From both the negative standpoint and the positive, habits are the result of repetition.

When recruits arrive at Marine Corps Recruit Depots, all they know is that they are arriving as a civilian and in thirteen weeks, they will be United States Marines. They have no idea what forcing functions will be put in place to create this transformation. The drill instructors, on the other hand, are fully aware of what it will take to transform these recruits into what the world knows United States Marines to be.

One of the first things that recruits must change is their attire. It does not matter if you have never worn boots or if you haven't cut your hair in ten years, before the sun rises the next day, all males will have their heads shaved, and all males and females alike will be in the same uniform. The first and last words out of their mouth will be sir or ma'am. They will wake up at the same time each day. They will eat at the same time each day. Their beds will be made the exact same way, every day or else…well, that's a story for another time. To be able to claim the title of Marine, you will be forced out of your comfort zone and given many things to keep you busy so that complacency doesn't set in. Trust me.

The point I'm making here is that it takes divorcing yourself from old behaviors and developing new ones to conquer comfort and complacency. Here are a few steps you can take immediately to get started. No, these steps won't have you Marine Corps ready, but you will develop personal habits needed along the journey to becoming what you desire to be.

1. Create a routine

Creating a routine is a great start to conquering those two deadly Cs. When you identify a routine that works for you, do everything in your power to stick to it. You can't break consistency and expect to keep getting the same result.

2. Get an accountability partner

Find someone you trust who will keep you focused. This can't be someone who has issues with either of the deadly Cs. Having the wrong accountability partner only increases your chances of falling to the deadly Cs. Having an accountability partner is important because we rarely hold ourselves to a standard the same way we would if we're answering to someone else.

Your accountability partner should be someone you trust and someone who has your best interest in mind and at heart. This person should be someone who will call you out if you slip. This person is someone who has value to you. Your accountability partner would be able to remind you of what it was you said you desired. This person will serve as your support system. They will be the person you will reach out to when you're feeling less than your best self, because that day will come.

3. Create Milestones

Establish milestones so that you can celebrate the small wins along the way. It fosters a positive mindset and fuels you to be able to continue striving towards your end goal. As you reach them, celebrate it like you won the lotto and move on to the next.

4. Take The Leap

You have to believe in yourself. You can only stay in the nest for so long.

You either get kicked out or you choose to make the jump…so learn to fly.

14

A Letter From That D Word

DEAR DIMYAS,
    I wouldn't do that. I don't trust it. It just doesn't seem as if this is the right thing to do right now. I've never let you down. Anytime I've given you advice you've stayed safe, so why deviate? I understand everyone is telling you that you should take a chance and pursue your dreams, but your dreams don't take care of your family. What takes care of your family right now is the job that you're in. Besides, how many other people have tried that? Do you really want to go and try to hack it as an entrepreneur or try to get a new job when you've already been at this one for so long? You know how you get when you meet new people. It's always uncomfortable, and you always feel judged. You deserve to be in a place where you don't have to worry about that, and that's here.

    What if you fail? Think about how terrible that will feel. Think about all those people who will watch you and ridicule you because you left something that was safe and secure. You don't need to deal with that stress. It makes sense for other people to try those things, but you are a person who likes to play it safe and that's a good thing. Think about the last time you tried something new. Do you remember how that felt when it didn't work out? These are the things I'm trying to prevent you from having to go through again. I need you to just trust me. Don't be fooled by the world telling you that you should go and shoot for the stars because they won't be there to catch you when you fall. I'm trying to protect you from that. Just think about it from my standpoint.

Love always,
Doubt

Doubt: a feeling of uncertainty or lack of conviction

Where does doubt come from? Many times, doubt comes from generational curses that you've yet to break. Perhaps you were told what you could and couldn't do growing up and some of those things have stuck with you. You need to address the roots of your self-doubt before you can move on. Besides, what purpose does it serve? None, when it comes to you fulfilling your purpose, other than keeping you in place.

That said, we must not forget about our gut instincts. Although this isn't what we are focusing on right now, doubt does have value in some cases. That gut instinct that triggers our spider senses also protect us from real danger. By the same token, we are naturally doubters after we have experienced things that didn't work in our favor. Many times we look at our past failures and highlight them so much that it prevents us from daring to take action again. It causes us to look at ourselves and our abilities to do something with a little more skepticism than before. This is an unhealthy mindset and it creates a self-defeating mentality, but you can beat this. No one knows you better than you. You have been your greatest supporter and greatest motivator. You have been with you through every up and every down. You are your own ride-or-die person, so believe in yourself.

Silence the chatter. Quiet the noise. In order to reach greatness, you are going to have to silence the senseless chatter in your mind. You need to get control over the mindless messages that doubt brings in, because they only cloud your thoughts and your judgment. What more are you willing to let slip out of your grasp because you're holding on to doubt? How long are you willing to go unfulfilled? You question whether you should take the new job, you wrestle with going all in on your business, and it is all because you allow doubt to have so much control. I am challenging you to do what sets your soul on fire. Pursue what makes you happy. Who cares if you don't make six figures? Some of the wealthiest people in the world are unhappy and unfulfilled; so don't chase money. Chase what fulfills you. Chase your purpose and the rest will come. You must start believing in yourself.

When doubt starts to creep in and that little voice starts to tell you that you should reconsider, the bigger voice needs to speak up and take full control of the situation. Do not give doubt a voice. Don't give it the energy nor the attention. You can strip doubt of its power if you drain it of the energy. It's about mastering your self-talk. It's about not allowing the negative thoughts to take control of your mind and prevent you from taking action. Positive self-talk is so important when it comes to you believing in yourself because it allows you to feel supported. When outside forces are not there to get you started, you need to have positive self-talk to help kick you into gear. Positive words of affirmation, motivational mantras, and good intentions need to become a part of who you are.

Believing in yourself is knowing that you're going to make mistakes and being willing to forgive yourself. It's not giving up on the person in the mirror. It's facing that person and saying, "I'm willing to do this for you because you deserve it." It means getting back on the bike even after falling. It means trusting that you can do what you said you would do despite anything standing in your way. Believing in yourself means finding more reasons why you can do something than reasons why you can't. It means doing a self-assessment to figure out how to get your strengths, talents, and gifts to work toward your advantage.

To get you started in killing all doubt, write out the top five attributes you have that can aid in you accomplishing your goals:

1. _____

2. _____

3. _____

4. _____

5. _____

Now I want you to take a second and think about each of the five attributes you just wrote down, the last time you used them, and how it made you feel.

15

You Do You

WHO IS THE person you dream of becoming? If no one was around to judge you, what would you do? Who would you become? Would you become the person that you've always wanted to be? Would you decide to take a chance on yourself and make the leap to do the thing you've always wanted to do?

What prevents people from trying to do these things anyway? Many people concern themselves with what other people's perceptions and reactions will be to them risking something new. But why? People on the outside do not matter. The only things that matter and the only people that matter are those closest to you. But as humans, we have become so accustomed to considering what everyone else thinks. We allow society to dictate what is right and what's wrong for us. This is not a healthy way to live. If you constantly worry and wonder what other people are thinking about you, you will never do anything for yourself. Here's a good question to ask yourself. Do the people I consider in my decision making process also consider my opinion in theirs? Most people only act the way they do out of the need and desire to be accepted by others. So when you finally do what you set out to accomplish, did you fulfill your dream or were you just fulfilling someone else's? That answer is most certainly the latter. Many people in today's world feel that the need to be accepted is more important than being true to one's self.

Oprah Winfrey said that our job in this lifetime is "to live to the highest degree of what is pure, what is honest, what is natural, and what feels like the real you. Anything less is a faked life." Too many people have fallen victim to what social media says they should look like, talk like, what music they should listen to, and what jobs they should work. The end result is generations of people being led by everything but their personal goals, passion, and purpose. Oprah goes on to say that "to be authentic is the highest form of praise. You're fulfilling your mission and purpose on earth when you honor the real you."

16

Stop Making Excuses

THE TIME FOR accepting excuses from yourself is over. No more making deals with yourself for not doing what you said you would do. You are no longer going to accept half-hearted efforts when you have the time and the ability to do what you've always wanted to do, but simply lack the will to follow through.

Would you ever accept $10 back when you asked someone for change to break a twenty? Would you ever accept a pizza delivery with only half the pie in the box? No, you wouldn't. Then why is it okay to accept half from yourself? Are you incapable of producing more? You must start requiring more of yourself because you are better than what you have shown. So what if you are tired? You are not the only person who has a kid that has kept you up at night. You are not the only person who has had a rough week. You are not the only person trying to manage classes and a job. None of that gives you permission to not follow through with what you said you wanted to do for yourself. People make excuses because their vision isn't clear.

A clear vision helps rid you of excuses. Vision helps you make sense of past mistakes. Sergeant Major James Cabarrus, USMC (Ret), speaks of elevation through reflecting on hindsight. One of the greatest teachers was yesterday. There are so many lessons to be learned from past experiences but we have to be willing to revisit them. We must view them as data, rather than failure. You should be willing to use those past experiences as stepping stones to elevate you to the next level. No longer is it acceptable to look at those scenarios and see them as things that just happened. It is important to judge every situation and treat it as if it all had a purpose, because it does. The purpose is for you to take those experiences and use them to better yourself. Every day of your life should be an opportunity to learn something new. You have been learning lessons your entire life. Lessons from success. Lessons from failure. It is time to get rid of every excuse we have made and start doing the work to make our dreams come true.

17

Kill the Comparison

WE'RE ALL GUILTY of it. Advertently or inadvertently, we all have, at some point in time, looked at what someone else had and compared it to our own situation. We've looked at some of the things they've accomplished and thought, "What if I did that?" We've seen someone driving our dream car, watched someone wearing the shoes or holding the purse we've always wanted and said, "What did they do to get that?" There are dangers associated with this. When your gaze is constantly on what others have, it will be impossible to appreciate what you have and where you are in life. In the world of social media, it is easy to get caught in this trap if you aren't careful. One of the dangers is when you start putting off what you desire for yourself to chase what you see someone else doing. You have to realize that the majority of what people post on social media is just their highlight reels. It is okay to look and admire, congratulate them and get inspiration, but when that inspiration turns to comparison, that's when the trouble begins.

So many people waste countless hours distracted by the next shiny thing someone has that they're unable to see what is meant for them. I personally want you to know that this is an unhealthy behavior and that what's meant for you is far greater. You're looking at the fact that they're driving the newest Benz and you're driving a Hyundai. They have a six-figure salary and you're barely getting by. You're looking at their six-bedroom house and wanting to be able to afford what they have, meanwhile you only have one kid and no need for six bedrooms. You're killing your ability to see what God has put in front of you because you can't stop looking in everyone else's direction. It is time to kill the comparison.

That shiny new thing may not be all it's cracked up to be. You don't know what sacrifices the person you're envying had to make to get that shiny new thing. You don't know if they put themselves in debt for the sake of looking good. Kill the comparison.

There is a cost associated with everything. That applies not just to material things. The great flaw of looking at someone else's relationship has led to the end of many others. People chase the proverbial knight in shining armor or look for their beautiful damsel thinking that's what they need to be happy, when in reality that knight or princess might not be able to show you the love you need. They may not be able to care for you in the way you desire. What is meant for you will be for you. Don't chase what others have. Identify what right looks like for you and have the discipline and the patience to trust that it will come to pass. Consider this: A knight in shining armor is someone who has never had their metal tested. When you've been through some things, that armor might have a few chinks in it.

Chasing what other people have moves you out of alignment with what your assignment is. Your assignment is your purpose. It is what you were born to do. Don't be blinded by someone else's light .

Comparing lifestyles has further consequences. Because we get so caught up in what other people have, we spend money we don't have on things we don't need. That then leads us to having to work the job we don't want with the boss we hate to make the money we need to pay for the things we only bought because someone else had it.

One of the truest sayings is that comparison is the thief of all joy. Don't make the fatal error of chasing someone else's false idea of happiness and success; instead, be ever reminded to create your own.

18

The Journey vs. The Destination

THERE ARE TWO types of people in this world: those who only want to get to the destination and those who take the time to appreciate the journey. I used to be the guy that when it came to road trips, all I wanted to do was pack the car the night prior, fill my tank up, and hit the road first thing. When I got on the road, there was no time for stopping unless my bladder was at full capacity. Although I had never been to some of the states I would be passing through, I wasn't really interested in stopping for the tourist photo to say that I've been there. I was all about getting to the destination. Then you have the others. The ones who will stop at every state line to get a picture. The ones who plan out the best restaurants to visit and research who has the best shakes in town. Those people, I'd venture to say, enjoy their trips a little more than I did, but I wasn't concerned about the trip. I wanted what was at the end.

In life, there will be those who care so much about the destination that they miss opportunities along the way, and there will be others who stop and smell the flowers along the way but maybe arrive a few hours late. Which one are you? Are you all about the journey or the destination? There are benefits to both ways of thinking. The person that cares about the destination can be seen as focused and driven while the one who cares about the journey can be viewed as easily distracted and wayward.

On the road to elevation, I would say the journey and the destination need to have equal importance. Life is too short to be focused solely on the end game but it's also too short for you to continue making pitstops. It is time to fill the tank up, plan your stops, stay on course and get to your destination.

19

Take The Stairs

OFTENTIMES WHAT STANDS in the way of us reaching success is that we want to take the easy way. We want to elevate but we don't want it to be laborious. We want to get put on a lift and glide our way to the finish line. We don't want to go through some of the rough spots that are along the way. But to truly make it worthwhile so that when you get to the top you can appreciate it, I'm going to have to ask you to take the stairs. I'm asking you to take the stairs because there are necessary steps you need to take and there are things you need to learn before getting to the top. Taking the stairs means appreciating each day for what it has to offer. The stoics of old offer wisdom on being anxious over nothing: the Roman philosopher Seneca once said, "But life is very short and anxious for those who forget the past, neglect the present, and fear the future. When they come to the end of it, the poor wretches realize too late that for all this time they have been preoccupied in doing nothing."

What I took from this was the lesson that every portion of life's journey has significant importance and each step along the way brings value to the equation. Everything we go through gives us information we need to make well-informed decisions, and with that information, we either continue on course or make moves in another direction. Without knowledge of the past, we are bound to make the same mistakes. Sometimes going back and repeating a process is for the better. There is nothing wrong with doing additional sets and repetitions. Besides, that is what builds muscle.

Many of us struggle with being able to appreciate taking the stairs because the world today promises everything quickly. Every commercial and internet ad says, lose this many pounds in seven days, gain this much muscle in two weeks, build this much wealth in thirty days, and all of it has created the "right now" mindset. No one wants to wait. Tomorrow seems like it's too far away. We want what we want and we want it now. The problem with this way of thinking is that sometimes we're so eager to move on that we end up filling our buckets with everything we don't need, so then when it's time for us to receive what is meant for us, we don't have the ability to see it or receive it because our buckets are already full.

What we need to start embracing is delayed gratification. We need to learn to appreciate the smaller accomplishments along the way, knowing that one day the thing you truly desire can be firmly in your grasp. It means sacrificing today for what you want tomorrow. We have to be willing to plant more seeds and trust that they will turn into a bountiful harvest without checking on it every day. Before you can reap a harvest, there is much work to do. There are steps you have to take. No farmer puts a seed in the ground and wakes up the next day expecting food for the table. Growing takes time.

The reward at the top of the stairs is the thing that you must keep in your mind, but you cannot make it everything. There has to be a balance. You can't be so focused on your success that you forget your family, your friends, or yourself in the process. Maintaining a healthy relationship with self and those you love is a key step. There is no joy in elevating to the top only to get there and look down at the family you've ignored or to look in the mirror and realize you haven't been taking care of yourself.

Each step you take on this journey brings you one step closer to fulfilling your purpose. Whatever has compelled you to start in the first place is still at the top screaming for you to get there. There will be many days when climbing the stairs is going to suck. In Hawaii, there is a famous trail called the Haiku Stairs or the Stairway to Heaven. The views from the top have compelled people from all over the world to come and make the climb. This climb leads to a view that you wouldn't be able to imagine. But here's the thing about this climb: it's all stairs, and it can be treacherous. Many people have reached the top, but there are others who have had to be rescued. Although they wanted to get to the top, many times the weather would prevent them from being able to do so and they'd end up lost or injured. On your personal stairway to heaven, there will be days when you feel as if you need to be rescued, but this is when you need to take a deep look within and remind yourself of what it means to finish the journey. Anything worth having is worth working for. Even if you get delayed. You must remember that a delay is not a denial, and with determination, you can do it.

Taking the stairs to get to success means you're going to have to address some things on the way up or they're going to bring you back down. You won't be able to bypass certain challenges and you shouldn't want to. Ignoring the pebble in the shoe during the climb can only last so long before it starts to affect everything else. What seemed like a small thing can easily become something major if you don't address it. By identifying and clearing out these rocks in the early stages of the climb, you eliminate things that stand in the way of what you really want, making it easier to commit all your conscious effort towards your dreams and desires. The stairs will test your stamina and make you question if this is something you really want, or if you are way out of your league, but here's the thing: it's supposed to do that. If something doesn't challenge you, it won't make you better and the reward in the end won't be as sweet. In order to come out the victor, you must be willing to weather every storm and still continue the journey.

- What small rocks do you have in your shoe that you need to get rid of before you continue?

- How do they affect you?

- What do you risk if you don't address them right now?

- What do you gain once you do address them?

20

Find the Champion in You

O N THE JOURNEY towards elevation there will be sacrifices you need to make along the way. Sacrificing in this case is giving up something that is important to you in order to have a greater chance of living a life of purpose and fulfillment. Of all the things one would potentially have to give up, time is the most precious. Time is something you can't get back and you don't know how much you have left. To sacrifice time means taking it away. You take time away from what you would like to do today to build toward what you want to be doing tomorrow. To do this, you have to put away the foolish things. Time with friends is a great thing if you are able to separate yourself when it is time to be productive. If you can't do that, then the sacrifice you have to make is to say no. You will also have to sacrifice time with family. I love my children more than words can ever describe but when it comes time for me to do things that require my full focus, I have to get away from them because my heart will always lead me to want to spend time with them instead. The end result of constantly postponing action is never finishing what I'm trying to do.

There is a mindset you need to have when it comes to sacrifice. If you only see sacrificing as giving something up, then you'll never recognize the true value of the sacrifice. If you see sacrifice as an investment, it makes it easier to see its value. With every good thing, there is the potential for it to have the opposite effect, and so we have to recognize the dangers. You know what they say: too much of a good thing can be bad. Therefore, you must know when to ease up as well. Too much time taken away from friends and family can start swinging the pendulum away from sacrifice and more towards neglect.

It has to be a balancing act, but the aim isn't perfect balance. If you think about a seesaw, when it is in perfect balance, there is no momentum. The joy comes from the ups and the downs. It is better to see less balance and more rhythm. Being able to understand the ebbs and flows that comes with sacrifice and managing them properly makes for a better journey. Understanding this is what separates regular players from those who become champions.

To become a champion means you will have to start doing something that is different from what you've been doing. You have to have the fighter mindset. No one can want you to succeed more than you do. It doesn't matter what coach is in your corner. It doesn't matter how many inspirational videos you watch. No one can make you a champion if you don't have the champion mindset.

When fighters are getting ready for championship fights, they go through grueling fight camps where they push themselves to the max. They have to completely change everything they do in regular life to put themselves in the best position to win. Fight camps are brutal. You have to train multiple times per day. You get hit more times than you can imagine. But here's the thing about all those shots you take: they prepare you for the fight that is to come so that when it arrives, the blows don't have that same effect on you because you are prepared. It takes a champion mentality to wake up the next day and say, "I'm gonna to do this all over again." You have to champion yourself to do it. Learn to be your own cheerleader. Don't seek praise or approval from anyone else before you seek and require it of yourself. Keep working at it.

How many hours do you think the great actors like Denzel Washington had to put in order to perfect their craft? How many times do you think he heard the director yell "cut" before he finished a line because he didn't get it right in the beginning? It is what he did behind the scenes that set him apart. He had to fight and he had to champion himself. We have to do the work behind the scenes. This means working at it in a hotel room, in the house, in the car. This means becoming obsessed with doing things right in the quest of reaching your purpose. The Marine Corps Staff Non-commissioned Officer Creed says it best: "Although perfection lies beyond the grasp of any mortal hand, I shall yet strive to attain perfection, that I may ever be aware of my needs and capabilities to improve myself." Finding the champion in you is not about attaining perfection, it is about continuously working to identify ways to improve yourself.

21

Elevation Requires Commitment

COMMITMENT: THE STATE or quality of being dedicated to a cause or an activity.

To elevate, you are going to have to become dedicated to your cause. To be dedicated to it means you have to believe in it enough to give it the focus and attention it needs. When you don't believe in something fully, it is easy to walk away from it. This is one of the main reasons I urge people to follow what sets their souls on fire and not what fills their bank account. It is much easier to commit to something that you're passionate about, that you can see yourself doing for the rest of your life, than something that just pays the bills. My favorite definition of commitment is "an engagement or obligation that restricts freedom of action." This second definition is so powerful to me because it makes clear that I am obligated to do what I said I would do and I don't have the freedom to go away from it. It is about living up to your own word. Inky Johnson said it best: "Commitment is staying true to what you said you would do long after the mood that you said it in has left."

Your relationship with commitment must be one that you are bound to. Of course difficulties will arise but that is just another opportunity for you to prove to yourself how badly you want it. It means whether times are good or bad, you will tough it out because you must do what you promised yourself you would do. I must remind you that commitments don't mean there won't be deviations. You can be committed to a destination, but there can be things and people along the way who cause you to deviate. The plan may have been to take your business partner all the way to the top with you but if things aren't aligning and there isn't a joint focus, you can stay true to your commitment of building a successful company without keeping the same partner the whole way. You must know who stands in support of your commitment and who or what oppose it. Philadelphia influencer, Wallace Peoples, better known to his followers as Wallo267, says that people fall into three categories: those who are helping you, those who are hurting you, and those who are hindering you. You must know who each of these groups of people are for you and where they stand in the grand scheme of things. If someone isn't helping you, it is imperative that you remove them from the equation because they have a direct effect on your ability to stay committed to fulfilling your purpose.

22

Your Freedom is Waiting
on Your Action

NDIA IS HOME to the largest population of Asian elephants in the world. In fact, of the thirty to fifty thousand Asian elephants in the world, more than half of them call India home. While many roam freely in the wild, there are some that serve other purposes for the people of India. One of the uses for these majestic creatures is tourist travel. Have you ever wondered how someone is able to train an animal that can weigh close to ten thousand pounds to be so docile and submissive? In some cases, trainers take young elephants and tie them by their feet to large banyan trees. (Banyan trees are some of the strongest trees in the world due to their deep roots.)

With their feet tied to the tree, the elephants always try to escape. They pull constantly in the hopes of freeing themselves but only grow more and more tired. No matter how hard the young elephants try, there is nothing they can do to free themselves from the tree and they eventually give up and accept where they are. It is at this point, when the elephants have been mentally broken, that the trainer gains full control over them. From this moment forward, the trainers can take the elephant anywhere they want with ease.

What's fascinating about this story isn't the fact that the elephants can be taken from the wild and trained to perform certain tasks. The captivating thing is that due to the training with the banyan tree, an elephant that has the physical ability to remove itself from whatever it is tied to, has now developed a psychological barrier that reminds it of being chained so it stops trying to get away and accepts where it is.

I share that story to ask you, what is holding you back? What do you have in your life that has you psychologically paralyzed and is preventing you from trying again? Some of you have been chained by something or someone for so long that you think you can't be free—but you can. Just because you were held there once before does not mean you can be held down now. Just as that elephant has grown, so too have you.

C. Joybell C says,

> "Some people live in cages with bars built from their own fears and doubts. Some people live in cages with bars built from other people's fears and doubts; their parents, their friends, their brothers and sisters, their families. Some people live in cages with bars built from the choices others made for them, the circumstances other people imposed upon them. And some people break free."

You're strong enough to break through. You're strong enough to try again. You're strong enough to walk away. Your freedom depends on it. Your freedom depends on your actions. I believe in you.

23

Are You Really Stuck?

THINK ABOUT THE things you've given more control in your life that you shouldn't have. The people you've entertained for too long. Those things and those people have become your perimeter collar. A perimeter collar is a tool that is used to train a pet not to leave a specific area. A dog, for example, will run in the yard and as it gets closer to the perimeter that you've established, the collar will begin to vibrate or give an audible beep. If the dog continues toward the perimeter line and reaches it, the collar will give a light shock.

Here's the thing about those collars. They work! On some dogs. Then there are other dogs that can get shocked time and time again, but they just can't help themselves. Their desire to get to the other side of that line is just too exciting to them. They don't know fully what's on the other side but they know it's something they want to see. Many of you have placed limitations on yourselves and at the onset of any discomfort, you willingly back up to where you're comfortable. You have to take on the mindset that nothing will be able to keep you contained any longer. You may face heavier shocks and you may want to turn back around but if you can push through that moment of pain, you will finally be free.

Are you willing to take that step? Many of the barriers you think you have are only mental. They are walls that can be broken down if you would just take a chance on yourself. Are you willing to cross whatever perimeter you have set or allowed someone to set for you? Are you strong enough to give it one more shot or are you too afraid of the shock? That shock may in fact be just what you need because some of your life's goals and aspirations have flatlined and are in desperate need of a defibrillator to shock them back to life.

Take a moment to write down three things that have been mental perimeter collars in your life.

1. _____

2. _____

3. _____

24

Breathe Life Into Your Fire

ONE OF MY guilty pleasures is watching the show *Naked and Afraid*. There is something about attempting to survive twenty-one days with no food, shelter, or water that captivates me. The best part for me is when I see a team that struggles to get fire because of the conditions they were in and seeing how the absence of this element affects their overall well-being.

If you've ever attempted to start a fire on your own, you'll quickly realize how difficult it is. Especially if you're naked in the middle of a wet jungle. There are three things that are needed to start a fire: oxygen, fuel, and heat. Whether you're using a fire starter or a bow drill, all the conditions must be right to get the flame going. When all components work together, the combustion becomes a fire. If any one of those three elements is missing from the equation, then the result will be different. This is often the case when the material they're using is too moist and the kindling does not get hot enough to cause a combustion. What happens then is that the smoke starts but it's either too wet or they can't maintain enough friction for long enough to get a fire going.

Having fire allows the contestants to boil stagnant water to make it potable. Fire allows them to stay warm at night. Fire allows them to be able to cook what they caught, and fire allows them to produce ash which is used to protect their skin from the outside elements. Without fire, rarely is anyone able to make it. But if they can get a spark, and if they can turn that spark into a fire, survival is possible. This is my favorite part of the show. When they hold the kindling in their hands and begin to blow, the smoke builds and becomes thicker and darker and just when they are about to give up—Voila! The flame appears and they have fire.

For many of us, the journey towards purpose and fulfillment has been just as difficult. You haven't had the best of conditions, you haven't had the best resources, but what you do have is an ember and the only thing you need to do now, is to breathe life into it.

Oftentimes what prevents the fire from starting is the environment. When the environment is not conducive to building a fire, then there are things that need to change. Your location may need to change. It may require you to go to higher ground. What does that look like in your world? What needs to change in your life? What people do you have surrounding you that are preventing the embers of joy, love, and purpose from being able to catch fire?

Before moving on, take a moment to reflect and write your thoughts about what you need to do to start or maintain your fire.

25

Abundant Positive Language

THERE ARE MANY ways to breathe life into a situation. The first way is through self-talk. Self-talk can be both positive and negative. Depending on which one you find yourself doing more of, will determine the outcome of many situations for you.

Let's start with positive self-talk. Is your positive self-talk like the cheer squad at a football game? For me personally, my self-talk changes based on the situation. If I'm working out and doing something that is exciting or if I'm sluggish to start, my self-talk sounds a little like David Goggins, Marcus Taylor, or Eric Thomas. What does your self-talk sound like? Self-talk is powerful. What you say and don't say can make or break your success.

Negative Self-talk

We're all guilty of it. At some point in time, we've all done it. Negative self-talk can be harmful if you are not aware of how often it is happening.

Here are a few examples of negative self-talk:

- "I can't do anything right."
- "I'm such a fool."
- "That's so stupid of me."
- "I always mess up."

- "I have never been good enough."
- "I don't even know why I try."
- "I don't have the skills."

If you have ever found yourself using this type of language, whether it's saying it out loud or saying it in your mind, the result is that your mental health and your well-being take a direct hit. As much as you may not like the way it sounds, this type of language is verbal abuse and the worst part about it is that it is self-inflicted.

The reason it is so important to control how we speak to ourselves is that we have the ability with our self-talk to be able to create positive and negative narratives based on what we're saying. As we chase our purpose, we must be cautious of inadvertently creating any negative narratives. So what, you failed? Now what? Is the plan now to just continue looking at the situation and reminding yourself of what you could have or should have done better?

An effective strategy to use when you catch yourself painting a negative picture is to recognize it the moment it begins and cut it at the root. You must remind yourself that you are bigger than the situation and that you can do whatever it is you have set your heart and mind to do.

Confucius says, "The man who thinks he can and the man who thinks he can't are both right." There is power in our words. With them, we will either continue to plant seeds of hope and prosperity or cause the ground to become infertile because of the toxicity of our thoughts and words.

"Be conscious of the self-fulfilling prophecy, whether you think something positive or negative, you unconsciously act in a manner that makes it more likely to occur." This anonymous quote is one of my favorites because of the gravity of what it says. Consider the last time you told yourself that something was not going to work out right. What was the end result? What about the time you told yourself you were going to pass a test? How did that turn out?

The self-fulfilling prophecy happens when the things we believe start to influence how we act on a subconscious level. In order to counteract this, we must use abundant positive language.

Abundant Positive Language

Abundant positive language is about saturating your thoughts with words that speak to prosperity, plentifulness, and growth. Growing up, the story of *The Little Engine That Could* was everyone's source of what abundant positive language looked like. "I think I can, I think I can, I think I can." Had it only been said once, that would be just positive language. The repetition is what made it an *abundant* positive language. In Indian culture, there are certain mantras that are recited 108 times. The reason for this is that the number 108 is significant to the culture. Among many things, the number 108 signifies the wholeness of the divinity, all Hindu deities, and in Hindu astrology, the twelve Rashis multiplied by the nine Planets is 108.

I am not telling you to say to yourself "I am great" 108 times. Although it won't hurt, I give you this information to help you see what repetition in abundance looks like. You don't need to travel all the way to India to see abundant positive language. You can make it a part of your regular vocabulary.

- "I am more than capable."
- "I am worthy."
- "I am strong."
- "I am my future."
- "I can complete whatever I set my mind to."

These are just a few examples of abundant positive language.

This is something positive we can do whether we are feeling up to it or not. I have come across many people who say things but their body language and their tone don't match. This happens when we don't want other people to know what's really going on inside. Some of the most successful people in the world have ended their lives because what was happening internally became too much to bear. These are the people who can benefit from your abundant positive language. Some people just need someone to speak life into them. Every single person on earth has an ember that is begging to become a fire and deserves to be a fire. All they need is someone to breathe life into them.

Abundant positive language is about changing the expectation in your mind. It isn't the absence of doubt nor the lack of fear, but the deliberate mental shift towards positive intention regarding a desired outcome. It is about getting rid of the expectation of failure. In John C. Maxwell's book *The Difference Maker*, he says, "Usually, the people who keep failing are the ones who expect to." Let that resonate for a moment.

The ability to use abundant positive language is based on your personal philosophy on life. If you are generally a negative person, then the chances of you seeing a situation from a negative standpoint would be greater. If you're a positive person, then more than likely, the majority of your thoughts are going to be positive. The question becomes, where do either of these mindsets come from? Are we predetermined to be positive or negative people? Do we have control of this faculty, or is this just an innate human behavior that we can't change? The answer is, yes, you can change it. Our brains are remarkably flexible and can change through repetitive effort. Due to its plasticity, the brain has the ability to continue developing long after our physical body has stopped. In the same way we can shape and strengthen our physical body through physical activity, we can exercise the mind to strengthen the brain too. In the process known as neuroplasticity, the brain forms and reorganizes synaptic connections, especially in response to new learning or experiences or following injury. When it receives the new stimulus through your efforts, new connections are formed while others are reinforced. It is during this process that new neural pathways are created to be able to change and create new habits.

The purpose of using abundant positive language is to build new neuropathways to be able to create the greatest version of self possible.

"As man thinks, so is he." —Proverbs 23:7

What we become in the long run will be the result of our thoughts and actions. Marcus Aurelius says, "The happiness of your life depends upon the quality of your thoughts: therefore, guard accordingly, and take care that you entertain no notions unsuitable to virtue and reasonable nature."

Abundant Limiting Language

More often than not, people who use abundant limiting language are those that find themselves in a perpetual downward spiral and have difficulty pulling themselves out of it. You must be mindful of the way you are treating yourself. We are often so hard on ourselves for where we are in life and for whatever reasons, we feel it is okay to talk down to ourselves. It is not okay. It is not acceptable to kill your own joy. You deserve more. You deserve to be able to look at your situations for what they can be and not for what they currently are. When you use limiting language, it stifles your productivity, initiative, and drive. The more you use this form of communication with yourself, the greater the effect it's going to have. In order to draw whatever we desire closer to us, we must cease the use of self- and situation-defeating language.

What we must start using is abundant positive language and the language of victory. We must make simple shifts in our vocabulary and the benefits will begin to manifest themselves. We need to change every "I hope it happens" to "I know it will happen because I have faith in myself and my abilities." Remove the "maybe" and the "probably" and make it "I will." Get rid of every "if" and proclaim "when."

The language we use with ourselves daily has the power to break through any mental, spiritual, and emotional chain that has kept you confined. You can have your breakthrough if you just break through.

26

Elevation Requires Change

I KNOW YOU JUST read that title, but did it actually register with you? For some of you, I'm sure it did. For others, chances are, it didn't. But, as we continue, you will see exactly what I wanted you to see and exactly how I wanted you to feel. If you could go to bed with the thought of what you want to become in your mind and wake up to it being a reality, would you do it? What if it meant some of the people in your life and some of the things you love the most would have to be left behind? Do you think you would be willing to give them up? What about that night out with the crew? Would it be worth it to you to cut back on your eating out allowance? Logically speaking, for me, it would be a no brainer. But that's looking at it through my lenses today. But would you do it? If your answer is yes, it means that you have the ability to make it happen, you just need to put the plan in place and do it. If the answer is no, then there are still some things you are going to have to address before you can elevate to the next level.

On the journey toward elevation, you cannot take any physical, mental, spiritual, or emotional baggage on the ride with you. Elevators can only hold so many people, hence why the maximum number of persons or weight allowance is always displayed. This limit is for your safety and the safety of all other passengers. Think about that when it comes to what you are going through. How many additional passengers have been preventing you from being able to elevate? How long will you continue to allow them to slow you down? By creating and following through with your plan, you will give yourself the opportunity to go to the next level. The next level means elevation, and elevation requires change.

The process of elevating means that you're going to go from the level that you are currently on and make your way towards the higher level that you want to reach. In order to make it to that higher level, many things in your life have to change. It is impossible to go up while staying the same. The first thing you have to do when you want to elevate is identify where you want to go. When you get on an elevator, you don't just walk in and stand there and expect it to read your mind and take you to your desired destination. You have to press the button for your desired floor.

Identifying that destination is the first step. So many people speak of going to higher levels and wanting to walk in their purpose but fail to identify what that level looks like. Not pressing your desired floor when you get on the elevator will just set you on an aimless ride going wherever other people want to go. Sadly, this is what life has looked like for so many of us. We have believed in everyone else and our lack of focus has caused us to get off on the wrong floor. I have personally done that in the past and I felt so foolish. And typically when it happened, I was distracted. Looking at this action from a real-world perspective, I lost focus on where I was supposed to be. Now I'm on the third floor when I wanted to stop on the second, and by the time I realize it, the elevator door has closed and I now have to wait for another chance. How many times have you stepped off on the wrong floor, worked the wrong job, or been in the wrong relationship?

When you don't know where you're going, when you don't know where you're supposed to be, when you don't realize where your true potential lies, it's easy to be distracted and get off on a floor that wasn't meant for you.

When you truly know where you want to go, you won't allow the simple things, those momentary pauses, to stop you from getting to your destination.

We must find our focus and stop following the latest trend. The best way to chart the course ahead is to sit with yourself and do an honest assessment of what sets your soul on fire. Ask yourself this question: What will allow me to walk in my true and authentic purpose? When you figure out what that is, guard it with your life and let nothing sway you to get off before your stop.

To elevate requires a little bit more than just identifying where you want to go. You know you want to go to another level but sometimes the elevator is full of other people who also have destinations that may be different from yours. This may mean you have to make more stops than you originally wanted to. Suppose your destination is the 12th floor. Floor 12 is success for you. Floor 12 is victory. Floor 12 is the marriage you desire. Floor 12 is the job you've always wanted. Floor 12 is a happy relationship with the kids. Floor 12 is mending past relationships and moving forward.

Now suppose you got on the elevator and the buttons for several other floors are illuminated already. There's no way to not stop there before reaching floor 12. If you think about it from a growth standpoint, these other buttons that are illuminated may be the stops that you need to make because you can't necessarily get to floor 12 if you haven't taken care of all the things that need to happen at floors 6, 7, 8, and 9. You might need to make some of these stops to be able to prepare yourself for what you're going have to go through when you get to floor 12.

There are steps that you are going to need to take to properly position yourself to elevate. There is training that you're going to need to do to be able to elevate. There is mindset development that needs to happen in order for you to elevate. There may be physical preparation you need to do to be able to elevate. And you may also need to shed a little bit of weight in order for you to be able to elevate. I'm not talking about physical weight. The weight I am talking about is mental weight that we carry that keeps us from being a better person. The things that weigh us down that we should separate ourselves from. The people that we should separate ourselves from. The things that we do that we should separate ourselves from. The procrastination, the laziness, and anything else that serves only to weigh you down.

Don't let elevator talk slow you down either.

Don't get caught up in someone else's dreams.

Too many times in life we get off at the wrong stop and we're forced to start over or wait because we made the decision that landed us in a place where we weren't supposed to be. All because the focus was off and we weren't paying attention, we've found ourselves working in places that weren't meant for us, working for and with people that aren't good for us, and in relationships with people we shouldn't be with.

For people to have the desire to change, there must be an event or sequence of events that drive them toward that end. John Maxwell says, people change in four different seasons:

1. When they hurt enough that they have to

2. When they see enough that they are inspired to

3. When they learn enough that they want to

4. When they receive enough that they are able to

Where do you find yourself right now? What junction of the road are you at and which direction are you going to take? It is time for you to identify where you're trying to go. Only you know where it is you're called to be. You know what you desire in your heart and mind. Since you know this, it is imperative to take the next steps.

Step 1: Take action

Just having the desire doesn't get you where you need to be. You must take effortful actions daily.

Step 2: Be prepared when it is your time

Are your eyes open to see the opportunity? Are you in a position to act? Will you?

27

Elevation Requires Help

WHEN IT COMES to elevating, sometimes you're going to need a little bit of help. Although you may be able to start the journey on your own, having assistance along the way to help you navigate will save you time, money, and heartache.

You have to be willing to ask for help.

There are two main reasons why we often don't ask for help, and both are killers of progress and I refer to them as E^2 (Egos and Emotions). These two things don't just affect us, they affect our relationships and our ability to succeed. You might know someone who has been there and done that, but ego will prevent you from asking that person for help so that you don't appear to be weak or lacking knowledge. You don't want to ask for help in this situation even though the other person has experience, but you need that help and they just might be able to provide a perspective that you weren't thinking about. They might be able to give you a tool that you will need in the long run. But they won't unless you ask.

You have to ask for help and you have to accept help. You can't make it to the top by yourself. You can't make it in the world of elevation by yourself. Tandem skydiving is a great example of this. You get to ride along with an expert and get the same experience. To be able to go through the experience alone would require many hours of training, time, and money. You can rid yourself of all of that by joining in with someone

ELEVATION REQUIRES CHANGE

who has already done it. Consider that accountability partner, mentor, or coach you're nervous about approaching for help to be your tandem buddy. You will be able to soar to higher heights much faster if you are willing to ask for their help.

88   The Journey Towards Purpose and Fulfillment

28

Carry Your Load

SARAH HAD ALWAYS been an athletic young girl. She could always be found climbing a tree or playing with some stray animal that wandered up to the house or that she met while out on her daily trek through the woods. The trail she would play on was about three miles long. She would go there with her dad and one day he saw her take off running as usual, but then she came back not long after. When she returned, he asked her, "Sarah, did you run the entire trail?"

She responded, "Of course, Daddy, but I stopped when I saw this bunny."

He smiled wearily, thinking they were about to add another pet to their growing menagerie. "That's really fast!!" he said.

Being a former runner, he knew she was much faster than the average kid her age. He asked her if she would mind running it the next day for time. Well, she agreed, and just like the day before, her time was fast—and not stopping for animals, her time was even better. Her dad asked if she would mind running track for the upcoming school year, to which she replied that it sounded like a lot of fun.

That fun then turned competitive as she and her supportive father began to see that she was faster than every student in her class. Sarah went on to win all of her regular season races. But things changed when she got to regionals. It was evident that there was a lot of work to be done when she lost the first round by more than ten seconds. Sarah grew extremely upset.

She was so mad, in fact, she decided she didn't want to stay and go for the lesser awards. Her father was very disappointed. No words of encouragement could get her out of the car and back on the track. They went back and forth over the rights and wrongs about quitting and for months she beat herself up over losing the race. He told her, "You can't just quit when things don't go your way. You can't always finish on top, Sarah."

Sarah stopped running for a bit and after a few months, her dad approached her about training again. He said he bought something that would help her out and make her better. It was a weight vest that allowed the addition of up to twenty-five pounds. She reluctantly agreed to start running again and put the empty vest on. She took off running, but her dad stopped her and placed a one-pound weight in one of the pockets on the vest and said, "Here's to carrying your load." She gave a look as to not fully understanding what that meant but continued on with the run.

The following day, her dad loaded more weight into the vest and once again sent her off, saying, "Here's to carrying your load." At this point the weight was slowing her pace down significantly and she was quickly getting more and more fed up. At the end of the run, she yelled, "I hate running with this stupid vest."

Her father looked back at her, smiled, and said, "Here's to carrying your load."

Week after week, Sarah's load got heavier and heavier. Her dad continued to add more weight before each run and sent Sarah on her way. On one of her last runs, he maxed out the vest.

Sarah was irate. She told him, "If this is what it takes to be better, I don't want to do it anymore. How many other kids are doing this right now?"

He pointed to the trees and said, "Here's to carrying your load."

Sarah stormed off in a fury. Running down the trails, she made it to the one-mile mark before her anger got the best of her. She went into one of the pockets and grabbed one of the weights. She yelled, "Here's how I feel about carrying my load, Dad!" and threw the weight. She went into another pocket, pulled out another weight, and threw it as well. Once she got to mile two, she took the entire vest off and launched it into the family pond before taking off in a frenzy back home. Her dad, as he'd done for every one of Sarah's runs, looked at his watch and noted her time. He quickly looked back up and noticed she no longer had the vest on. She runs right past him into the house. He gives chase right behind her, asking, "What happened to the vest?"

"I threw it away and I'm never wearing that stupid thing again." She continued yelling, "Why did you make me do that?"

He replied, "It was to make you better."

"Make me better?! Dad, I've run slower every run and you think this made me better?"

"You're better because you now realize you have a choice," he continued.

"What choice do I have?" she said.

"The choice to carry your load or shed it."

In life, there will be many trials that you will have to face. There will be many setbacks and failures. It's human nature to feel down because of a failure, but you don't have to hold on to those weights. You don't have to carry your frustrations. You don't have to carry your failures. You don't have to carry the depression. You don't have to carry the hurt. You don't have to carry your load. Shed your load and run your race.

What things have you been carrying for longer than you should have? What are you allowing to weigh you down? What will it take to get you to start removing some of the weights out of your vest?

Holding on to the past blocks your happiness.

When your hands are full with the weights of yesterday, it is impossible to receive the blessings of the present.

It is so much easier to operate with a lighter load once you shed the heavy things in your past.

Many people have to carry heavier loads because of their circumstances and that is understandable. What is not acceptable is when you have the ability to shed some of it but choose not to. So many things make us feel like we have to hold on to the weight of the past, and one of the heaviest loads we carry is pride. Shed your load.

29

Skill + Will

FAILURE TO MOVE often has much to do with a lack of competence, confidence, and will. When a person has the required level of knowledge to perform any task, rarely do they hesitate to act. Knowledge carries with it confidence but only after repetition. This competence and confidence I speak of, let's just call it skill. For those who lack competence in any area of what they set out to do, there will be a level of reservation that makes them hesitate. They hesitate for many reasons. Perhaps they don't want to let anyone down, or they're afraid of facing embarrassment, or they simply aren't in the position to be vulnerable. For this person, as long as they have the will, they can learn and develop the level of competence needed to excel. I have noticed that you can break people down into three categories: those who have skill and will, those with will but no skill, and those with skill but no will. I think it is safe to say that this applies in every aspect of life.

For those who have the skill and the will, everything they set out to do is based on what they've envisioned. It can and will be done. These are people who rarely ever make excuses. They accept responsibility for their actions and they are driven toward mission accomplishment. They are self-starters. Their skill isn't the only thing that ensures victory for them, it is their will that makes them win out in the end. They recognize that they have the ability and the tools and they put them to work.

For those who have the will and no skill, these people are eager to learn. They are willing to admit what they don't know so they can become proficient.

They too have a high level of self-awareness and a greater understanding of the need to manage it. What they lack in skill, they make up for in will. They are willing to ask questions. They are willing to make mistakes. They are willing to be vulnerable. Once they learn the skill, these are the people who go on to be some of the greatest teachers because they have empathy and see the value of teaching, communicating, and working together towards a common goal. It is the will to learn that sets them apart.

As for those who have the skill to perform yet don't have the will to work, these people become the cog in the wheel. These are the people who knew how things were done at one point in time and did it well, but now rest their hats on that. They lack initiative and will typically perform when it benefits them, and not necessarily when it benefits anyone else on the team. These people have the ability to be great but their lack of motivation holds them back. You find individuals like this in every field of work. Athletes who are good but never become great because they aren't willing to do what it takes to up their will to increase their skills. Entrepreneurs who have incredible ideas but don't have the drive and discipline to continue developing their craft. It doesn't matter how much skill a person has. If the will is lacking, the performance will be too.

The skill/will concept isn't anything new. Enlisting in the military requires minimal skill, but it requires will. It requires the will to learn a new discipline, a new skill, new rules, new lingo, and more importantly, it requires service members to be willing to sacrifice not only their time, but potentially their life for a greater cause.

Where do you sit in these categories?

In the journey towards purpose and fulfillment, your ability to work towards perfecting your skill is crucial. In addition to that, you must develop the will to continue pushing forward despite any setbacks.

30

Prepare For The Climb

NOT MANY OF us likely know the name of El Capitan. But to climbers, the mere mention of this three-thousand-foot-tall mass of granite sends chills down their spine. Situated in Yosemite National Park, El Capitan is considered to be one of the most challenging climbs in the world. The level of difficulty increases exponentially when a climber desires to free solo the route, meaning to climb it without the assistance of any safety gear.

Meet Alex Honnold. The year is 2017, and he is prepared to take on this feat that many consider to be impossible. Alex Honnold is considered to be one of the greatest rock climbers of all times. His love for the mountain face led him away from the safety of academics to the open rock walls where he finds peace and tranquility in what others see as fear and uncertainty.

How did he get to be who he is today? He didn't just wake up one morning and start climbing mountain faces. You don't get to this point without doing the work behind the scenes. Honnold prepared for years before eventually deciding it was time to tackle and conquer El Capitan. What made his journey more incredible than those who did it before him was that he was going to attempt to do it with no ropes and no safety gear.

The years leading up to El Capitan were full of both mental and physical preparation. He made everything that was a part of the climb priority. He stretched, he strengthened his grip by hanging by just his fingertips daily, and he went over every inch of the rock face in as much detail as possible.

This preparation was needed because there were crevices of the rock face so small that they could only be gripped with a thumb.

Everything he did was with a purpose, and it was the purpose of not only reaching the summit but doing it in amazing fashion. Before attempting to climb the route, Honnold and his team did safety checks on the rock face where they cleared and cut away debris that could prevent a safe climb. After this process was done, he then climbed with ropes and safety gear to make sure he was fully confident at every step of the way. When he finished the rehearsal climbs, he was meticulous in his note taking and studied them to ensure nothing was missed.

When questioned about his thoughts about El Capitan before climbing he said, "Each year I would show up and it would seem just much too daunting. To walk up to the base of the climb without rope and harness, it just feels a little outrageous. Getting over that side of it was the hardest part."

This is one of the many lessons to be learned from Honnold. This is what we must realize in our lives. It is not that we should have no fear. It is about recognizing your fear but having the courage to follow your passion and pursue your purpose regardless of what is standing before you. Honnold said he would go to the base of the mountain and say, "I know that I'm in danger, but feeling fearful while I'm up there is not helping me in any way, it's only hindering my performance, so I just set it aside and leave it be."

What people don't see when they look at those who have accomplished amazing feats such as free soloing El Capitan is the preparation that goes into it. No one that has achieved great success has done so without extreme levels of preparation. Everyone that has made it to higher levels of fame, notoriety, and greatness has had innumerable mountains to climb. They have slipped more times than they can count. The calloused hands of those who have worked, toiled, and grinded in the dark in pursuit of their summit will never be seen, but it was done. How many times do you think Alex Honnold lost his grip? How many times did he have to figure out another way? Before setting a record, what doubt did he have to get rid of?

It is time to set fear aside and let it be. Fear is a tool that you don't need.

What is your El Capitan? What are you going to do to prepare for it? You don't have to tackle it today, but you do need to start planning and preparing for it. It is time to do your research about what it is going to take to climb up that rock face. Epictetus said, "How long are you going to wait before you demand the best for yourself?" Time is up for watching people walk in their purpose and you not starting.

Demanding more of yourself is not about doing something that isn't within the scope of your abilities, but about giving yourself the best chance possible at fulfillment. Demanding more of yourself means pushing the envelope when it comes to gaining knowledge.

If you're an athlete it means running an extra mile or doing one more drill.

It means waking up a little earlier if you know your days get busy.

I am not advising that you go to the extreme. Too many people have popularized the idea that never sleeping is a good thing. Yes, you need to make sacrifices, but the sacrifices you make never need to be a risk to your mental health and well-being. Preparation, time management, and commitment are some things that not everyone is able to stay consistent with, but that must be learned if you ever want to be able to ascend to greater heights.

Many years ago, while in Japan, I had the opportunity to hike Mt. Fuji. I started my trek at the base of the mountain where most tourists start. Everything was perfectly fine. The temperature was great for the time of year. Around three hours into the hike, my body started to feel different. The altitude started to affect the way I performed. I didn't realize what was happening because I was in great shape and due to the nature of my job, hiking wasn't out of the ordinary. The issue wasn't that I was out of shape. The issue was that I was not prepared for the challenges that came with the altitude. Over time, I realized I was starting to experience what is known as altitude sickness. Altitude sickness, if you're not careful, can kill you, and if it doesn't kill you, it makes you delirious. I can tell you right now, I started feeling delirious when I looked up at how much more I had left of this mountain to climb.

Although I was super excited and mentally prepared to go on that hike, I truly was not prepared for the climb. In our journey toward elevating, you will need to be sure you are prepared for the climb. Preparing for the climb is different for everybody. Preparing for the climb as a college athlete who wants to be able to go pro could mean making sure that you're doing what you need to do academically. Making sure that you're keeping your grades up, that you're hitting the gym, that you're eating the food you need to eat, that you're getting the sleep that you need to get. Preparing for the climb for a teacher could mean something completely different. For a teacher, preparing for the climb means getting ready for the challenges associated with curriculum, testing, administration, and depending on where you are, dealing with complexity of working with underfunded schools or inner-city kids. Preparing for the climb as a brain surgeon doesn't just mean that you graduated medical school. It means that you have to constantly be in the books. You have to stay ahead of the latest research and techniques. Preparing for the climb is different for the UPS and FedEx driver just as it is for the airline pilot. Everybody has necessary steps that they need to take to ensure that they are ready and able to accomplish the things that they set as their true desire and intent.

You prepare for the climb by taking inventory of what you have so you can identify what you need. If you don't need the extra equipment (people, negative thoughts, past failures), don't take them with you. But you will need your safety equipment (mentors, coaches, faith, purpose) to get to the summit.

On the road to elevation there will be many setbacks, pitfalls, trials and tribulations, and the way you prepare to handle those things will determine how quickly you can get to your target destination.

You will be knocked down, and that's when you need to have the right tools, equipment, and people most. Even if it's just one person, you have to have that support system. Although you can make the climb alone, it'll be a lot easier if you don't. Having somebody who can help you get through those highs and lows will make the climb a smoother and more enjoyable experience.

31

Are You Prepared?

"**I**'M THE BEST! I'm the best! I'm the best!" Normally stoic in her gaze and minimal with her words, this was the phrase Rose Namajunas repeated as she walked down the aisle to face the reigning strawweight champion Joanna Jedrzejczyk. Joanna was known for getting in her opponents' heads before the fight, and it worked every time. Not only was she able to defeat them mentally with her witty remarks, enhanced by her fierce stare and Polish accent, but she would beat them physically in dominant fashion when the bell rang. The betting odds said this fight was going to end just as the others did before, with Joanna taking the belt home again, making it her sixth successful title defense. But Thug Rose, as she's known, had a different end in mind. Barely three minutes into the very first round, the fight was over. Rose Namajunas shocked the world and was crowned the new strawweight champion. How did she get there? The short answer is preparation, but there was nothing short about the journey getting there. Despite life's many ups and downs, Rose Namajunas persevered and came out the victor.

Abraham Lincoln said, "Give me six hours to chop down a tree and I will spend the first four sharpening the axe." The preparation period is where we must all sharpen our axes. This is the time when you smooth your stones and ready your bows. It is not during war when the battle is at your doorstep that you prepare, but during peacetime. You don't show up to the audition and ask to see the script. You prepare beforehand so that you can put forth your best self when the spotlight shines on you. You study the playbook so that when the coach calls you into the game, you know your routes. You can't scream for doors to be opened for you only to get there unprepared. Winston Churchill said, "To each there comes in their lifetime a special moment when they are figuratively tapped on the shoulder and offered the chance to do a very special thing, unique to them and fitted to their talents. What a tragedy if that moment finds them unprepared or unqualified for that which could have been their finest hour."

What does preparation look like for you? Are you setting yourself up for success? Are you planning with a purpose? Are you making a detailed plan with contingencies if something doesn't go the way you desired?

Years ago, when I was doing bodybuilding shows, cardio was the hardest thing for me to do. Although it was not physically challenging, the act of actually getting on the machine to start a cardio workout was the thing I dreaded the most. So what I decided to do was put my shoes on the treadmill. Call me crazy, but my treadmill was located directly beside my bed. I did this because each morning it forced me to make a decision. I either had to make the conscious decision to walk away from the treadmill knowing my shoes were right there or I could just get on and make it happen. It was almost as if every morning I woke up, my shoes were looking at me saying, "We're ready if you are. We've been waiting on you."

In 2016, I had the privilege of being one of the first Marines to design the new physical fitness job for the Marine Corps. Our team was made up of some of the best Marines around the Corps and two of the best athletic trainers and strength and conditioning specialists around. Although we all came from various backgrounds, we worked as a unified team and the end result was the formation of the Force Fitness Instructor Course.

While teaching these courses, there was a common theme we noticed with the students when it came to teaching sprint mechanics. We would always tell them to get in their sprinter's stance without guidance. When they were all told to get set, you could tell who was formally trained, who was athletically inclined, and who had two left feet.

In the line-up you could see everything from people being in a four-point stance as if they were playing football, to people in sprinter stances with a long back leg, even some people standing straight up as if they had never run a day in their life. Then there would be the others. The ones with their feet one in front of the other, hands down on the pavement, waiting for the command to take off. Every last one of those people waiting at the start line knew what they were about to do, but there were only a few of them who were in the right position to do so. To be able to run the best race possible, you are going to have to position yourself properly. Are you positioned for success? The way you position yourself determines if you are prepared or not.

Preparation and positioning go hand in hand, but they are not the same. You can be prepared but if you never step out and try, you'll never be in position to do anything. How does one put these together? You build a bulletproof plan. That is, one that has contingencies should anything go wrong. As we say in the military, no plan survives the first shots of combat. You can't stop the unknowns. This is the reason why you develop more than one course of action to ensure you can continue to maneuver towards your objective.

32

Protect Your Garden

GROWING UP THERE was a garden in my backyard that my grand-mother started. She cared for that thing like it was one of her children. No matter how late she worked, she'd come home, change out of her uniform, and head straight there. She put her heart and soul into it. She would spend countless hours tending to it. Whether it was watering the plants or adding fertilizer, she was meticulous about everything she did. She made sure before the day ended that every part of the garden received the attention it needed. As the plants grew, I vividly recall watching her going outside to get what was ready for harvesting with the most satisfied look on her face. Her look was the only satisfied one, because surely mine wasn't. I knew I'd have to help clean it all before cooking it. One thing that always stood out to me in the process were the vegetable leaves that had holes in them. The first time I saw the holes I asked my grandmother if the leaves were still good. She was quick to remind me that just because the bugs had a sample before us didn't mean the food wasn't good. She told me no matter what she did, there would always be bugs, and as long as we washed them well, there was nothing to worry about.

As an adult, I look back at those moments and think about how my grandmother's lesson applies to real life. Every single one of us has a garden. The gardens of our mind. That garden is either one that is out in the open or it is one that is protected and set up in the form of a greenhouse. Of course this greenhouse isn't one where we are planting things physically, but without a doubt, planting is happening every day.

Every day there is something that we are planting in our minds or allowing someone else to plant. What's being planted is everything you consume. Through the things you watch, the music you listen to, the company you keep, and of course the actions you take.

The goal is to start treating our minds like our own little greenhouses. Protecting it from harmful outside influences. Not allowing weeds that can hinder our progress and our success to come in and crowd what we actually want to grow. You have to choose what you will allow to grow in your garden. When you don't have that garden protected, it is easy to have seeds of doubt, worry, fear, and procrastination set in. Those are the weeds.

While traveling in Tennessee, I visited a close friend of mine on his family farm. As we walked the grounds, he started talking about the importance of controlling the weeds in his garden. He said for many people, walking past one weed doesn't mean anything because they can always get it the next time, but to him, it has to be plucked right away. The reason for this is that weeds compete with everything around it for nutrients and, because they grow so fast, they will rob your plants of the vital nutrients they need. Not only do they go after the nutrients, they compete for sunlight. After robbing plants of both food and light, the end result is a garden that will die.

Here's what's worse about weeds: they drop an abundance of seeds. Knowing this, you must kill the abundance with abundance. When the negative thoughts try to fill your mind and rob you of light and attempt to suffocate your dreams, the use of abundant positive language can help you clean up your mental garden and put you on a better path of healthier thinking. If you don't, the threat of the weeds growing and taking over your mental garden becomes imminent.

If those figurative weeds aren't removed, they will suffocate the life out of all of the things you do want to grow there. Your dreams can easily be overtaken if you're not creating a greenhouse for your mind. Inside that greenhouse you should be growing passion, love, joy, and happiness. You should be focused on keeping everything that isn't in line with that out. When life begins to happen, we tend to not pay attention to the smaller things creeping in. Things like envy, greed, selfishness, or on a personal level, fear and regret.

My grandmother didn't have the ability to build an adequate greenhouse to ward off insects that were destroying the plants. We have that ability in our minds. We have the ability to control what thoughts we allow to germinate and sprout. If we focus on positivity, that's what we will produce. We can't allow the small things to get into our heads. Once they get there and take root, they begin to suffocate our joys and hopes. We must be careful in our daily actions to build a greenhouse for our thoughts. We must be ever conscious of what we allow to affect us. Everything that affects us that's not controlled will eventually infect us if we allow it.

To dwell or to ignore. That is the question. Dwelling is not pulling the weeds.

The more you allow yourself to dwell on something that isn't contributing to you going to the next level, the more it will become a part of you and the more it will affect performance. To allow toxic thoughts to take up residence in your mind is a sure way to stifle your progress. These are the weeds.

You can't sit and look at the problem because that changes nothing. The more you ignore something that needs to be done, the greater the problem it becomes. It's the check engine light that has been on for a while. The longer the light is on, the greater the potential for damage to the vehicle.

In order to combat this, you have to constantly check on your mental garden, like my grandmother tending to hers, to ensure you're on the right track. You must be conscious of everything that is taking place no matter how small it is. Checking in with yourself daily is the key to your victory.

Who or what has been robbing you of the nutrients you need? What weeds are in your mind? What will it take for you to begin clearing them away?

I would ask that you start now. Start clearing away the mental clutter so that when you start your journey towards your purpose, you don't have anything holding you back. You don't have past issues haunting you, reminding you of the last time you failed. You don't have that one negative family member in your ear telling you to stick with what is safe. It is time to kill it all. Uproot it and scorch the ground and place a barrier between the weeds and yourself so that they can't return.

33

Preparatory Command

THE PREPARATORY COMMAND is something that is used in military drill movements for marching. When the senior member is ready for the troops to execute a movement, they give the preparatory command. The preparatory command is designed to let everyone know what is to come. If a commander wants the troops to face to the right, then they would say "riiiiight" as the preparatory command.

They don't move until the commander gives them the next command which is the command of execution. In this case, the word to make them move would be when they say "face." After the command of execution is given, it is then that the troops take action, executing what they were just prepared to do.

Moving before the command of execution isn't allowed. This isn't just the case in the military. If you look at track and field athletes, they also have a preparatory command and a command of execution. The preparatory command there is the word "set," and there is no movement allowed until the gun goes off, which is the command of execution.

You never want to anticipate the command. What this means in life is that we don't need to anticipate the command of execution, but you need to be prepared for it. This is being ready for the opportunity when it presents itself. This means doing whatever needs to be done to line yourself up for the thing you want most.

It is time to give yourself a preparatory command and to stand firm in that spot. It isn't time to allow your mind to wander off. There is no time to think about anything other than the mission at hand. When you're at the position of attention, your hands are by your sides and your head and eyes are straight to the front and you're waiting for that next command to be given.

What makes this situation different from any other is that you personally are your own commander of troops and it is up to you to give yourself the command of execution. You have to give yourself the permission to act.

Don't delay.

Here's the thing about standing at the position of attention. When you stand at the position of attention too long, you get fidgety. People start to get frustrated. If you're standing at the position of attention and you lock your knees, you're going to pass out. This means you cannot just stand there for too long after being given the preparatory command or something is going to happen. It is when people stand in the same spot for too long they begin to lose focus.

It is never a good thing when there's too much delay in between the preparatory command and the command of execution. The delay makes you second guess what you wanted to do. The delay leaves room for things to creep into your mind that throw you off course. There isn't much time between when the pitcher starts the pitch to when the batter should start the swing. To close the gap between preparing and executing, you must address the things that have been delaying you from being able to accomplish what you set out to do for yourself. You told yourself there were new moves you wanted to make, you told yourself that you wanted to create something. Yet from the time you told yourself you wanted to do something, from the time the idea popped up in your head to now, there has been too much delay.

What is it that makes us so slow to start? Growing up, I remember lining up to race my friends in the neighborhood. We would all get in our set positions and we would be chomping at the bit to start. One of us would say, "On your mark, get set..." and every single time we raced somebody would jump before the "go." So we would reset. And after we were reset, somebody would jump again. No matter how many times we did it, no matter how many times we reset, we would always have someone jump the gun. The reason why they jumped the gun is because they were so excited to win that race—and they knew they had the ability to win it. Some of you know you have the ability to win yet you still are not putting yourself in position to take off. It's time to get back to the starting line and prepare to run your race.

On your mark, get set…GO!

34

The Switch

A FEW YEARS AGO, while teaching at a leadership academy, our students had the opportunity to switch roles with the instructors. We had previously instructed them on how to conduct proper physical training sessions from start to finish and it was now time for them to demonstrate proficiency by constructing and conducting their own for a grade. Some of the sessions they came up with were challenging and others needed work.

I remember one in particular that was put on by a smaller Marine. He gave the brief on what he wanted everyone to bring for the workout but gave us minimal details about the session. All we knew was we had to wear a pack that was supposed to be thirty-five pounds and we were going on a run. The next day we came in, weighed our packs, and made our way to the starting point. The run started off at a decent pace. Not too slow, not too fast. After about mile two, I started feeling a little different about this session. I was so used to being the instructor and knowing the run route, knowing when it would end and how hard I was going to push them, that I forgot what it was like to be on the other end. We made it to the halfway point, which I estimate wasn't more than 2.5 miles, and the Marine instructed us to put our packs down. As instructed, we took our packs off and did a series of exercises without gear on. When we finished, we were told to grab a pack that wasn't ours. We'd be finishing the run with the new load. I started thinking to myself, "What's the purpose of that if we all weighed our packs and we all have the same thing inside?" Not one to show my emotions, I smiled, gave a motivated "Oorah" (Marine motivation call) and grabbed the last pack available. This pack belonged to the Marine who was conducting the session. When I grabbed his pack and attempted to put it on my back, I had to add a little more "umph" to it. His pack was noticeably different from mine.

After getting the pack on, I tightened the shoulder straps, and we continued the run back. While running this time, the Sergeant began to talk. He started talking about things that hit home for me. He started saying how he knew some of us were outside our comfort zones. He said he could see our bodies started to show signs of discomfort. With every "turn here," a new degree of difficulty was added to the run and with every turn we made he continued to talk. The conversations that took place in the beginning of the run have diminished and all that could be heard was the sounds of boots hitting the ground, heavy breathing, and the Sergeant quoting Vince Lombardi, saying, "Fatigue makes cowards of us all." He started explaining that when there's no adversity, people are willing to do any and everything. When there's no threat in front of you, people will willingly step up to the challenge. Jumping across a small ditch with the pack today doesn't seem as easy as the day before without a load. When fatigue hits, people start doubting themselves and their abilities.

After the run, I started thinking about what took place. Everyone was told to come in with a pack that weighed thirty-five pounds yet his pack was at least double the weight of mine. I took that experience and started to look at it from a real-life perspective. Everyone, including you and I, go through things that challenge us. It's so easy for you to look at your personal situation and think how bad it is and how no one else can be feeling the way you feel. The reality is there are millions of people who are going through things far worse than you. Imagine being able to make a switch with someone in the race of life. Would you be willing to carry someone else's load?

During that switch, I learned a valuable lesson. I learned that life is about appreciating what you have. It's about not comparing yourself or your situation to anyone else. No matter what pack you're carrying, your personal journey to greatness will challenge you, but if you own the weight you carry, if you recognize your struggles, you can and will be victorious in the end.

35

Getting To Success Sucks!

THERE IS NO clear-cut path to success and you won't get there without facing adversity. The journey towards success, if I'm being totally honest…well, it sucks! In order to be successful, you have to go through what others aren't willing to go through. You are going to be forced to endure things that you never thought you would be able to endure, but if you can continue to run this race despite everything standing against you, if you can "embrace the suck" and make it through this time in your life, I promise you, success is going to feel better than you could possibly imagine. Success is going to taste like you never thought it would taste. It is going to be the best thing that you've ever had.

I had a successful career in the Marine Corps and it was not because I was willing to do everything everybody else in the Marine Corps did, it was because I did all the things that people did not do. It was because I chose to push my body to the limits. It was because I chose to have a healthy lifestyle when it came to my nutrition. I took pride in caring for my body as if it were my weapon because, in reality, it was. What I put into it needed to be things that would benefit me in the long run. What I consumed in food was to assist me in performing at my best. What I consumed mentally was to allow me to provide more than what was expected of me to my seniors, peers, and subordinates. My success was because I chose to look at the people who were succeeding and identify what they did that would fit my agenda and help me get to where I wanted to go. Getting there wasn't easy. There were many sacrifices that had to be made and this is what makes the journey to success suck.

To go up, you must give up. We have to stop being satisfied with good and chase great. You have to be willing to get rid of some things in order to reach higher heights. You have to get rid of everything that slows you down. Are you willing to separate yourself from the partying and drinking? Can you see yourself changing the people you hang around? Are you willing to put aside hobbies that steal your time?

Before I truly committed to change, my productivity would diminish from August until late January. Why? Because it was football season. How many die-hard fans do you know who will never miss a game if their favorite team is playing? I'm guilty of it. I'm a Roll Tide kinda guy, and if my team was playing, I was willing to stop everything to make sure I didn't miss a single play. Everything was planned around the Alabama game. If I had to do homework, shop, cut the yard, or clean the house, everything was done before the game started or it was postponed so that I could watch the game uninterrupted.

When I started to take my own advice and look at the things that were slowing me down, I began to see that I valued watching other people chasing their dreams more than I valued chasing mine. Let that sink in. When I first said those words, it hit me like a ton of bricks. That realization made me start making Dimyas Perdue priority number one. No longer would I spend all day Saturday and Sunday watching the games and not doing anything for my mental and physical health, and not another day would pass when I would root for anyone louder than I rooted for myself.

Imagine if you wanted a personal victory just as much as you wanted your favorite team to win. How hard would you scream for you? You can make this a reality if you truly desire to, but understand this: you will be treated like an outcast. The minute you start making yourself a priority, others will notice the distance and they will call you on it. Are you ready for that? Are you ready for the ridicule that comes with being a buzzkill because you'd rather study instead of hanging out? I was willing to accept being judged. I was willing to accept being labeled. I was willing to accept being misunderstood.

It takes that to get on top. When you put yourself first, you'll start to receive the success you've been longing for. The promotions will come and new positions will open up for you. You will be elevated above your peers. Your business will begin to thrive. You will start to elevate, but—listen to me closely—nobody is going to put you in a position of authority if they haven't seen that you can make the sacrifices needed to be in that position, nor are they going to reward you with a position of authority and leadership if they don't think you can take care of people. You won't get the starting position if you don't show up on time and put forth your best effort every day.

Can you withstand blow after blow? Can you and are you willing to weather that storm? The answer is yes. It is going to suck trying to get to greatness, but you can do it. The path to success is paved with many failures and you will encounter many setbacks, but I know you have what it takes to continue. **I believe in you.**

36

Getting To Success Isn't Always Fun

T HIS TIME FELT different. As I packed my bags to leave the house for my second trip to the cabin to write, I felt an overwhelming sorrow come over me. I started to feel selfish. This was far from the emotions I'd felt the first time. The first go around I was crazy pumped up. I knew it was something I needed to do. I was excited. In that moment, it was a feeling of pride that I was forsaking comfort to pursue greatness. It was only going to be five days and I knew it would be worth it because there would be no distraction. It was only going to be five days and I knew it would be worth it because there would be no distractions.

But how was it so different this time? I was only set to go for two days, but the emotions associated with this trip were different. I felt like I was leaving my family. I felt like I was being selfish. My daughter held me a little longer this time and told me she didn't want me to go and that affected me. I told her it was only two days and that this was something I needed to do.

Even her reaction was different this time because the first go around when I told her I was going to the cabin so that I can create a legacy for my family, her first response was that it wasn't for the family, it was for me. She didn't say it with malice in her heart, but that was how she felt. It hurt. But instead of walking away from that, I addressed it head on and reminded her of her personal goals and what it was going to take to accomplish them as well as what it was going to take for me to be able to accomplish mine. Judging by her reaction as I was walking out of the door, she fully understood this time.

I packed my last go bag in the truck and started to drive off and there stood my bride with my young son in her arms. She said, "Tell Daddy bye and you'll see him later," and as he stared at me driving away, he started to cry.

Moments like these have the ability to do a few things. They can inspire you to really kick things into gear or they can affect your emotions in a way that make you decide to put things off again. For me, it was the first of the two. It meant sticking with the promise I had made to myself and those I loved and not letting anything cause me to deviate. There are far too many things in my mind that I wanted to be able to share with others and if I didn't, I'd not only let myself down, but I would have stolen time away from my family, no fruit would have been produced by those efforts, and you wouldn't be reading these words right now.

There are so many people who have great ideas but are not willing to stay true to their word to make it happen. It sucked leaving my family for a handful of days just as bad as it sucked having to deploy. Why? One of those I had no choice in and the other I did.

Are you willing to step away from what you love to accomplish your goals? Dave Ramsey said, "Ideas are a dime a dozen. People who execute them are not." I am not willing to go to my grave as one of those people who didn't execute and neither will you. You will execute because you are going to take your ideas and not allow them to stay in a box. It doesn't matter how many times you have to start over again. It doesn't matter how many times you get ridiculed or told that there's already someone who does that. Who cares if someone else is doing it? You can do it too and it just might be better. So what if they tell you they don't think you're smart enough? None of those things matter. What matters is you believing in you and knowing that you will finish what you started. This is all a part of your story and your journey. No one ever started from scratch and didn't hit a road bump. You have to keep showing up every day, keep giving it everything you have plus some, and keep defying the odds. Getting to success won't always be fun, but my money's on you.

37

Defining Moments

THERE ARE MANY moments in sports when what the audience witnesses seems like something out of a movie. June 13, 2019, the NBA Finals between the Golden State Warriors and the Toronto Raptors, is one of those moments. Before the first game of the finals, there was a lot of talk about how the Raptors were out of their league and it would take a miracle for them to pull off wins against the Warriors. People then went on to say that if they won, they would not have the same success if they were to play them in their home stadium. Game one came and as expected, there was a lot of doubt about whether the Raptors would be able to defeat the Warriors, but they did. They went on to beat them at home as well. Ultimately, the Raptors won the NBA Championship.

There were many moments that led to the Raptors winning the National Championship but there was a defining moment when Golden State had the opportunity to win but they called a time out with none remaining. This caused them to receive a technical foul, which in turn gave the Raptors a chance to shoot two of those coveted free throws mentioned earlier, and that sealed the game. If you look at life as a series of defining moments, you will see that there are many opportunities to succeed but that success depends on your reactions in those all-important moments. The defining moment for you may be a final in school. The defining moment for someone else could be the sales presentation they're supposed to give to market their product. For a doctor, the defining moment can be anything from the sincere look in their eyes showing a family they're in good hands or the clamping of an artery that saves someone's life. In order to be better for ourselves, for those we love, and those we are to lead, it is important to take full control of life's defining moments. Don't leave it to chance. Put your heart into it. Make the decision to act and give it all you've got.

38

Prepare To Be Told No

AS MUCH AS you want to hear a yes every time you go out, rejection will undoubtedly come. It's okay to be told no. I've been told no countless times, and you will be too if you're on a mission to live out your purpose.

In 2006, I was screened and selected to become a Marine Corps Recruiter. This was by far one of the most mentally challenging duties I had ever been given. What made this duty so challenging was that I was no longer surrounded by other Marines like I had been at a traditional unit. Instead, I found myself in the heart of Louisiana with a mission of finding qualified men and women to serve by my side. This sounds like a great story on the surface but recruiting during the middle of Operation Iraqi and Enduring Freedom, as well as being a little over a year removed from Hurricane Katrina presented numerous challenges. What I was prepared for was being in front of people. That was no issue. What I was not prepared for was being told no by teachers, students, and parents who more often than not, had one or two words before it that they felt I needed to hear. My success on recruiting duty hinged upon my ability to receive that no, overcome indifference, identify drawbacks, and show how the Marine Corps could aid in transforming any-one into the person they truly desired to be.

I did this well. My first year on the duty, I was meritoriously promoted in rank, I received numerous recruiting awards, and I was placed in charge of a recruiting station. To be able to accomplish these things meant not taking no for an answer. I was given a mission, I understood it, and nothing was going to stop me from accomplishing it. I couldn't have done it without creating action steps and following through. I didn't receive their NO as a rejection, I saw it as an acronym meaning New Opportunities. By being told no, people helped me to rely on my knowledge and skill set to identify their needs and explore new opportunities with them.

Whenever you are faced with a no and you are pursuing what you know is meant for you, I encourage you to see it as a new opportunity. That job you didn't get may not be the ideal job the creator has for you. That relationship ending could be the one that makes room for the love of your life to arrive. When you are told no, I beg of you to not give up. Continue putting your all into your next step and try again. Try as if your life and future depend on it, because they do.

39

Delayed, Not Denied

WHEN I WAS younger, all I wanted to become, all I dreamed about, was being able to make it to the NFL. I didn't want to make it just to say I did it; my main motivation was so I could put my mom in a house. This was truly a life goal for me. It didn't happen because of some of the foolish mistakes I made along the way and the career paths that I chose after making those mistakes. I then had to make a decision about what I would do to set myself up to be in a position to one day fulfill the promise that I made to my mom. Keep in mind, I have yet to fulfill that promise but I will.

The purpose of me sharing that story is to remind you that although you didn't accomplish what you set out to in the beginning, as long as you have breath in your body, you have the ability to continue pursuing it. Too many times people sit and lament about things they wish they would have done when they were younger, how they are too old to be able to do those things now. Sure, at forty years old, chances are I am not going to the NFL to be a starting running back. (Although I still have juice in these legs!) After growing up and doing some further reflection, what I realized about my dream is that it was never about me making it to the NFL. My dream was about me being able to purchase a dream home for my mother. The NFL, to a child, was the mechanism that would afford me the opportunity to do it the fastest. As an adult, I know there are countless ways to be able to make it happen, but my mechanism of doing it now is by using my gifts. So my dream hasn't died, it was merely delayed, and a delay doesn't mean a denial. You have to work your way through.

"A gem cannot be polished without friction, nor a man perfected without trials."– Seneca

What are some the dreams you thought were denied that are only delayed? Write them below:

_____

_____

_____

_____

_____

_____

40

A Letter To Greatness

DEAR GREATNESS:

The thought of you gives me chills. When I think about what it would be like to reach you and what it would be like to say that what I desired for us has actually become reality, I become overwhelmed with emotion. I am like a kid who for the first time stands atop the highest mountain and gazes out on the open land, feeling as if I were a king and nothing could stop me. Feeling like everything that lies before me, as far as my eyes could see, I could have it all.

But not if I don't work for you. Not if I don't put in the time and effort for you. I recognize you and I could never be one if I'm not fully dedicated to doing everything that needs to be done, and not just doing it but doing it to completion. Doing it with my whole heart. Getting to you is not going to be as simple as I used to think, but I know what it requires now. You want to see sacrifice. You want to see action, and I am willing to show you. I know I'm not the first person to chase after you and I know I won't be the last. But the difference between me and everybody else is I am willing to run the race and even if I grow tired, I will never give up on getting to you because I know what I want.

I understand that there will be ups and downs, peaks and valleys, sorrows, and triumphs, but I'm in it for the long haul. You are worth it. Forgive me for not showing it long ago but at that point in time in my life, I was not capable of understanding who you were and what you meant to me but now

I do. I don't care how long it takes, how many miles I have to travel, how many hours of sleep I need to lose preparing to get to you—I will do what I have to do. Greatness is what I am chasing and greatness is within me. We are destined to be one.

Love always, Dimyas

When I speak of greatness, I don't want you to confuse that with fame. When I speak of greatness, I mean taking charge of your future and owning what is to become of it. Greatness to you could look completely different than it to does to me. For me, greatness is a healthy family that is rich in love and a home that is blessed. Greatness involves the impact I am able to make through my words and my actions. Greatness to me looks like someone believing in themselves more after interacting with me than they did before. Greatness is my words echoing through history long after I leave this earth. Greatness to you may be watching all your children sitting around the dinner table with healthy hearts and minds. Greatness to me looks like someone getting back on the horse and trying to ride again despite being bucked off. Cowboy up! Greatness to you may be graduating Summa Cum Laude. Greatness can mean being the first millionaire in your family. The first CEO. The first author.

It is time for you to reach and exceed everything you desired. Your planning and building season only lasts so long. You've been developing for years. It is time to go be great. No matter what it is to you, greatness is possible. Your greatness can only be achieved by you, therefore you should be the only one to define it.

41

Vision

MARTY'S EYESIGHT HAD never been as bad as it was getting lately. He first noticed the changes in his vision in his thirties. He would find himself squinting at things more than he used to. His wife told him that he should really consider reading glasses. After constantly being told to "stop squinting or you're gonna get wrinkles," he decided to take her advice. He made an appointment with the local optometrist. Upon his arrival, as with every other patient, they conducted an eye exam. Marty was asked to read the smallest line he could see. He chuckled and said, "E." This was funny to him because, as we know, that is normally the single biggest letter at the top of the chart. He went on to complete the test as well as the rest of the exam. After that, he was asked to pick out a set of frames. Perusing through the collection on the wall, he tried on pair after pair in front of a mirror before settling on a set that he thought suited him best. Two weeks later, he received a call to pick up his glasses. When he got there, he took the glasses out and stood in front of the same mirror where he had tried on all the frames before. Only this time, he could see that there was something written on the base of the mirror. Written in small letters across the bottom were the words "It's not that I wasn't here before, you just didn't have the ability to see me."

Marty's poor eyesight in this situation represents not having a clear vision in life. It could also represent looking at life through a negative lens. When you look at things through a negative lens, you are limiting the things you can see. When your lenses change, you are much better able to see situations more clearly. Seeing is also about positioning.

Someone asked me what I thought the difference was between a rich mindset and a poor mindset, and my immediate response was exposure. What people are exposed to has the ability to either inspire or stifle. The beauty these days is technology gives people a chance to see almost anything in the world, but what's behind a screen only lasts as long as it takes to scroll to the next video. If you can take someone and expose them to greater things, they'll never be able to unsee that. They'll be like Marty reading the line at the bottom of the mirror and saying to themselves, "It's not that these great things weren't here before, I just didn't have the ability to see them."

Our vision determines our position, so we have to be careful about who is adjusting our lenses. Your vision can be changed by everything you see, hear, and do. Have you ever been around someone who is always happy, full of energy, and never seems to have a bad day? What is it like to be around them? How do they impact your mood? If it's at work, how does that energy impact your work performance? More importantly, how does it impact their work performance?

Well, what about the opposite? Have you ever been around Negative Nancy or Pessimistic Pete? What does that do to your mood? A friend of mine recently told me about someone he was considering ending a relationship with because no matter how many times they spoke, the glass was always half full, and someone was drinking the rest. He described it as emotionally draining. Not only is a person like this draining, but if your perspective on life isn't fully developed, it can warp your lens and change how you see the world. If you aren't where you need to be, their mindset can begin to influence your outlook.

Have you ever tried on someone else's glasses? What did it feel like? I love when my kids would first try mine on. Their reactions were almost as if they were staring into the sun. What I needed to help me see clearly was simply too much for their eyes. What my prescription allows me to see is what's best for my vision.

We all have different origins that make us see life the way we do. Our individual outlooks have been shaped by the people who raised us and by our social network. Not everyone is meant to be able to see what you see. Likewise, their prescriptions aren't meant for you nor will they ever be. You shouldn't aim to see things exactly as they do. If their viewpoints make your situation better, then borrow those lenses. If they don't, then it is best that you stick with yours because the headaches associated with a bad prescription will make you regret it.

My life's vision is something that is meant for me, just as yours is meant for you. Many times we go through things and the purpose of those events is to help shape who we are to become. You can look at life's unfortunate events as the things that happen to you or you can see them as the things that have happened for you. Everything I have gone through in my life has shaped me into the person I am today. Without those events, there is no way my outlook on life would be what it is because the experience of facing those challenges have made me think and act the way I do.

Life's positive and negative events have helped shape what I see and have given me the vision that I have for the future. A glorious future that I can't stop imagining and won't stop imagining until I get it. And when I do, I will set my sights on something else because my personal journey toward greatness doesn't end when I accomplish one goal. I will chase greatness until my time here on earth is done. And even after that, my vision is that through these words that I write, my message will be able to live on long after I am gone.

One thing we must be aware of is that there's a difference between seeing and vision. Seeing is being able to recognize what is in front of you. It is the sense of sight. But vision, for the sake of purpose and fulfillment, goes beyond seeing to enlist the imagination. Vision is dreaming. Your vision is tied to your why. Your why is tied to your purpose. Why are you here? What are you destined to become? What have you been created for? Your mission is to find your why and chase it with passion and vigor until you make it a reality.

42

Problems or Possibilities

"ALL RIGHT, THEY'RE on our left, they're on our right, they're in front of us, they're behind us. They can't get away this time." These were the words uttered by one of the most decorated Marines of all time, Colonel Chester "Chesty" Puller.

Chesty gave us tons of great quotes. The quote above is one that not many people would ever have had the guts nor courage to say. During this fight, Chinese forces had him and his men surrounded at the Chosin Reservoir, and death for Chesty and his men was imminent due to the overwhelming firepower and size of the enemy forces. But there was one thing this legendary Marine had that his Chinese enemies didn't. He didn't just see problems, he also saw possibilities. He'd go on to say, "We've been looking for the enemy for some time now. We've finally found him. We're surrounded. That simplifies things." If he would've focused only on the problem, the entire division would've been wiped out. What he did instead was change his outlook on the situation. By doing this, they were able to create a plan that ultimately led them to victory.

If you're one of those people who has trouble seeing possibilities because you can't see past your problems, there are a few things you can do. The first is to stop admiring the problem. Focusing on the situation for too long can lead to many negative things if no actions follow the thought. Some of the best advice I ever received was to look at a situation and ask this question: Can you do something about it? If the answer is no, then don't worry about it. Don't dwell on what you can't change. If the answer is yes, the answer remains the same: don't worry about it. If you have control over something, then why stress over it? Create a plan and attack it. Admiring the problem does nothing but highlight the negative. You can move forward if you start searching for possibilities.

Another tool you can use is what I like to call the optometrist method. If you have ever had an eye exam, you'll know that after the normal chart test happens, the optometrist sits you in a chair and brings the phoropter (vision machine) towards your eyes. Your job is to stare at the object in the center as the optometrist makes adjustments. With each adjustment, the optometrist asks if the object in the center looks better or worse, clear or blurry. If it looks worse, they continue to make adjustments until they've found the ideal lens prescription that best fits your eyes. My recommendation for anyone going through a situation where they have trouble seeing possibilities over their problems is to simply make small daily micro-adjustments to their thinking. By doing this, the problems will become the blurred image in the rear and the possibilities become the clear image in the center.

43

Blinders

THE KENTUCKY DERBY is by far the most prestigious horse racing competition there is. The horses that race are, without a doubt, some of their owners' most expensive and prized possessions, as they should be. Especially considering the amount they pay for them. On the low end, you have the 2009 winner Mine That Bird that was purchased for $9,500. At the top of the chart is the year 2000 winner Fusiachi Pegasus that was bought for $4 million. Now, I know what some of you are thinking: there is no way I would pay that much money for a horse. For the average person, that's true, but for someone who desires to earn millions of dollars from that purchase, the potential return on investment is worth taking the shot. But with horses, there is a real gamble. If you don't know anything about horses, let me tell you, they are easily distracted and startled. Because of this, horses are given what they call blinkers or blinders that go on the side of their halters to block their vision of what's beside them and behind them so they don't get distracted by those things. The blinders forces them to only look at what's in front of them. It's absolutely necessary for the horse to wear blinders in order to have any chance at winning. I share this with you because of the applicability of it in our world.

Not every day of our lives is a race like the Kentucky Derby; however, we are in a race involving the highest of stakes. Just as the owners have made large investments in their prize horses, you've made an investment in yourself, and because of that, it's time for you to put your blinders on. It is time to focus on closing the gap between what it is you want most in life and what you have now. It doesn't matter who is running beside you. It doesn't matter if they are trying to do the same thing you're trying to do. Sure, someone may have a better pedigree than you. They may even be smarter than you. But that should not stop you from chasing excellence. Don't let the outside influences affect your race. You must put your blinders on and start running.

By that I mean you have to remove the outside influences from your view. When you shift your focus entirely to what you desire, subconsciously you start to move towards it. It's the same thing as driving. If you're in the driver seat and you're distracted by something on the side of the road, inadvertently the car starts veering towards where your gaze is. This is one of the many causes of secondary accidents. It happened because your vision has shifted away from what was in front of you, to something that didn't matter. Why do we spend so much time focusing on things that don't matter? On people who don't matter? So much time is wasted on trivial and meaningless things that if we were to add it all up, who knows how much time we have lost that we will never get back. It was all because we didn't have our blinders on and lost focus.

In order to elevate, you're going to have to keep your eyes on the target and keep taking shots. When I first put my blinders on, it wasn't easy. I would sit down to write, and it seemed as if that was the moment when everyone in the world would suddenly want to call me or text me. And what would I do? I would answer it. Why? Because I am a people person and I thought, "They're calling me because they need me." And because I cared so much, I would put myself to the side and I would listen. Thirty minutes later, I'm nowhere near the end of the conversation and I haven't made any personal progress. So who benefited in this situation? In the beginning, I said it was both of us. After all, these people are important to me. But then when I looked at the years that had gone by and I didn't have the degree I said I wanted, the book wasn't written, and I wasn't any closer to any of the other goals I'd set for myself, my answer changed. Maybe the blinders were on, but I wasn't focused on the end goal in front of me. I was still turning my head to look to the side and stopping to look behind. I wasn't running my race.

You can still be a nice person with blinders. Just know that when you have the blinders on, it's go time. That's not time to scroll through your phone or watch television. That's not time to go to a party. That's not time to go out to dinner. Those times will come after you have hit your objectives. While the blinders are on, you need to focus on the vision because your vision will influence your behavior and your behaviors will determine the quality of work you produce. The blinders are there to help you set healthy boundaries.

If you're surrounding yourself with people who aren't driven, don't think for a second that it's not affecting you. It may be subtle, but someone is leading and someone is following. Someone is setting the standard and someone else's new standard is being created. If you want to be successful, then the people you spend the most time with should be pushing you towards success, not pulling you away from it. If you're going to have a circle, it needs to be a circle of people who want you to win and are willing to do what it takes to get you there. Napoleon Hill called it the mastermind alliance, or as it has been said in recent times, the mastermind group. Hill described the mastermind group as being "two or more people who work together for a definite purpose." The group around you is akin to the horse's jockey. The jockey has raced before, knows the destination, and will push the horse at the right time. During pivotal moments in your race, you can leverage the strengths of your mastermind group (i.e. their education, influence, and experience) to help you see your vision through. They can help you stay focused and you will need it at times because there has never been a racehorse that could put the blinders on themselves. This close group can help you get to your destination and give you the push you need along the way to stay focused on your vision. If your gaze starts to drift, your path will too. If you let your focus shift to others, then it will always be others who get the glory, but if you focus on yourself, then all of your wants, through your focus and discipline, can become what you have. It is all about staying focused on your vision.

Dr. Myles Munroe said that there are two types of visions: natural vision and heart vision. Natural vision is what we see in the literal sense. Heart vision is tied to a purpose. He said, "Vision from purpose is tied to your destiny." The significance between natural vision and heart vision is that each of them has the ability to influence the other. If all you focus on is what you can see immediately in front of you with no thought to the future, you will be easily blown off course. Heart vision, on the other hand, can help you set your eyes set on a something and keep them there. When the heart has a true vision, the desire to chase excellence becomes greater than the many other things competing for your attention.

44

Competing Interests

I WOULD BE LYING if I said it was easy to not lose focus, especially since I have already mentioned how many times I have started and stopped in my journey of elevating toward greatness. There are countless things that are competing for our attention day in and day out. They have taken my time, they have taken my efforts, and they have captured my thoughts. But I realized that everything I wanted to do was blocked because not only were my thoughts captured, so was my ambition. I became content. I became happy with watching other people live out their dreams on social media and I stopped making efforts to reach my own. How many of you are in this same position? How many of you recognize where you are but haven't found the drive to make the change?

Myron Golden calls the cell phone the electronic income reducer. We spend so much time glued to our phones and distracted by them that we become so easily blinded. What starts out as just watching one video someone sent you turns into you scrolling down a rabbit hole. Now you've gone from watching a video of a cute baby dancing to shopping for supplies to start your next DIY project.

Everyone needs an outlet. It is hard to be on 24/7. So what you need is to find an outlet that aids in you being better and not staying the same. We see the latest shiny thing and we head toward it. Every day there's a new dance you can learn to go viral. Every day there is a new group coming into town that you must go see. Sure, going to the concert once is not that bad.

Neither is going twice. But when you look at the totality of those events and calculate the number of hours you spend dedicated to everything else, the data speaks for itself.

On the one hand, you tell yourself this dream is what you want, but on the other hand, your actions say otherwise. This is a result of losing your drive due to competing interests. This is the result of having no clear agenda and allowing outside influences to rob you of your passion. The competing interests have extinguished that spark and have taken your initiative. So, what do you do to get it back? It is about doing things in increments and being relentless about it. Small daily contributions towards goal attainment. Whatever you want to accomplish must be tied to a purpose or else it has no real value. You must work diligently toward the goal you've set for yourself. Simply working towards a goal is different from being relentless. To be relentless means being persistent and unyielding. It means not easing up. It means not taking your foot off the gas.

45

Be Relentless

WHEN YOU ARE truly ready to elevate, you will be relentless in your pursuit of personal greatness. I knew I was truly on my relentless pursuit when I started to look at everything I was doing, all the people I was talking to, and every influence I was allowing to come into my life. I started to ask myself questions in the middle of these interactions: What value does this add to me? If it doesn't bring any value to me or to my goal, then why in the world am I entertaining it? It wasn't that I was being rude. I never spoke or asked these questions out loud, but the more I started to have these thoughts, the more I began to value my time and who I gave it to.

I became fully aware of my value. I became more conscious of whom I allowed to have my time and my energy. I began to use an analogy that came to mind about the cell phone and its battery life. Most people plug their phones in every night so that when they wake the next day it has a full charge. When the cell phone is fully charged, you know you can communicate with who you want, whenever you want, and for a good amount of time because you have a full battery. Things become a bit more complicated when your battery starts to run low. When you're at 10%, you are a bit more cautious about going on social media. You are careful about how long you're on a call and you most certainly won't answer the phone if it isn't someone that holds value to you.

I started treating my life this way. Instead of giving my energy away to everyone just because, I started to guard my energy (time, skills, abilities) like I only had 10% remaining. I was careful about who got any of that from me because I realized people would continue to take if I continued to give, and for the sake of me and my goals, I needed to make myself a priority. By doing this, I could finally begin to see what it was going to take to walk in my purpose and get to the top.

Even after you get on top, you still have to be relentless. Don't think for a second there isn't someone else with the same dream you have. Look at sports. The minute the starting player gets hurt, there's the eager back up who is ready to go and has been relentlessly preparing for this moment. What you must remember, whether you are on your journey or you have made it, is that the wolf on top of the hill is never as hungry as the wolf climbing up.

In 2003, a story started of a pack of wolves climbing up with the intent of taking over the hill. When Sir David Brailsford joined the British Cycling team, there was not much to brag about. He had recently become the performance director of a team that hadn't won anything major in over a hundred years. That would soon change, but there was a lot to do first. In order to improve their performance, he began researching as many process improvement techniques as possible to identify ways to make the individuals, as well as the team better. After doing his research, he came up with his "podium principles" which were made up of strategy, human performance, and continuous improvement. These principles were designed to make small micro adjustments (increments) in all facets of their lives. The human performance aspect included how they slept, what they ate, how often they would wash their hands, and what they would and would not wear to name a few things. With strategy, they painted the floors white to be able to identify any debris that could contaminate the bikes and hinder peak performance. They also looked at the members of the team. They assessed where they all were as a baseline and looked at what it would take to get them to the podium. If the gap between where they were and where they needed to get to was too wide, then it was decided the juice wasn't worth the squeeze and that person was not placed on the competition roster. Every day, the goal was to continue making 1 percent increases in every area. The goal wasn't to race a minute faster. It wasn't to lose five pounds. The goal was to increase by 1 percent. It was about the aggregation of marginal gains. Within a period of five years, the wolves had made it to the top and they were unstoppable. They were consistent and they were relentless in the pursuit of their 1 percent increments, and it led to winning three Tour de France races and sixteen gold medals between the 2008 Beijing and 2012 London Olympics.

None of us have a Sir David Brailsford to track our progress down to the last detail, but this is still something you can do for yourself daily using the same approach he did with his team.

Step 1: Identify Your Dream

Where do you want to end up? This is a question you must continue asking yourself. What does happiness look like to you? What is your purpose? When you can answer these questions, you are ready to begin the next step. Without a vision in mind, it will be difficult to plan effectively.

Step 2: Set Targets

Break down your big dream into smaller action items and set your sights on those targets. Make the 1 percent changes to get towards your target, be relentless in your pursuit, and learn to see the value in making incremental steps towards your goal.

Step 3: Make Minor Adjustments

The small changes you make over time will be the major accomplishments in the months and years to come. Be consistent is your efforts and be sure to never diminish the value of marginal gains.

46

Your Dream, Not Theirs

WHEN WORKING IN your purpose, you will find that you are there when you are using your natural gifts. It may also mean you will need to unearth your gifts that have been buried. Gifts that have been buried because of past hurt. Gifts that have been buried because of past failures. You must stop allowing the greatness within you to be destroyed by outside influences. Not everyone deserves to know what your plans are because not everybody supports you and wants to see you succeed. Stop sharing your thoughts and your gifts with everyone. There are people who will celebrate your failures but never celebrate your success. This is why it's important to get comfortable with being alone because on the journey toward your purpose you will lose a lot of people along the way. So get comfortable with being alone.

Sometimes loneliness is needed. You are pursuing your purpose and you are pursuing your dreams, not theirs. No one is going to celebrate your dream in the beginning because it isn't theirs. They cannot see what you see and they cannot feel what you feel because your vision is yours. People won't understand why you lose sleep at night over it because your vision is not meant to be viewed through their lenses. It is meant for the world to see when it is done. You will need to be driven to the point of being viewed as mad. You will have to show them. You will have to be determined and be willing to sacrifice . Only then can you make your dreams into reality.

Nothing great comes easily and true elevation is going to take everything you have and then some. There will be setbacks upon setbacks. There will be times when you will doubt. There will be many moments when you question why you began in the first place but if you just remember why you got started and look back at your true purpose and the value that will come from you achieving it, you will stay on course and you will stay on the path. Failure will make you doubt your purpose. What's worse, those who warned you against starting will point out even the smallest errors and you will be foolish enough to believe them. Don't let someone else's fear stop you from starting again. Your race isn't over. It only appears to be over if you treat it as a sprint and not a marathon.

You're on the path to fulfillment. You are on a mission to fulfill your destiny, so don't quit just because you missed the mark on your first try. Too many people set goals for themselves and give up right away.

You cheated on the diet then quit.

You failed the test so you dropped out.

You tried communicating with your spouse but they didn't put in the same effort and so you gave up.

Imagine if the greats of the world like Michael Jordan quit after missing the game-winning shot. What if Thomas Edison gave up on the light bulb? What if the Wright brothers refused to try again? If they had given up, it would have affected life for everyone for generations to come. Kalpana Chawla was an Indian American aerospace engineer and the first female astronaut of Indian descent to go to space. She was well known for her roles around the Space Shuttle Columbia mission as well as many other great contributions she made to the field. She once said, "The path from dreams to success does exist. May you have the vision to find it, the courage to get on to it, and the perseverance to follow it."

Many times we encounter a little adversity, and it becomes a barrier to performance. But if we can remember the vision, take courage, and have the will to persevere, we will be able to reach our true purpose in life.

47

A Letter To Fear

DEAR FEAR:
  I'm so sick of you. I am sick of wanting to do what I desire to do and consistently having you hold me back. Who exactly do you think you are? You don't own me. You never have and you never will. For a moment you may have thought that and you know what? I thought you did too. But you don't. And maybe it's my fault. Maybe because I didn't stand up to you in the beginning, you felt it was my duty to do as you said and just stay in my lane. But not anymore. Do you know how much time I have wasted on you? Do you know how many opportunities I've missed that would have been in my grasp if I had simply gotten over you sooner? It's always negative with you. "What if you fail? What if it doesn't work out?" You said those things to keep me right where I've been. How foolish I was. How naïve. I should've known better. I am so over you just showing up whenever you want to disrupt my peace and derail my train. I'm over making plans for the future and then have you shoot them down the minute I mention them out loud.

  What's worse about this entire thing is that my grandmother had to deal with you, my mother had to deal with you…but my sons and my daughters will not. There will be no more guilt trips. There will be no more of you making me feel as if what I bring to the table has no value. This ends with me and it ends today. Fear, you have no place in my life and as of this moment, you and I are done!

Thanks for nothing,
Dimyas

Fear is defined as an unpleasant emotion caused by the belief that someone or something is dangerous, likely to cause pain, or is a threat. Fear also stems from the threat of physical, psychological, or emotional harm. This harm can also be an imagined harm. The imagined harm for me is the strongest of them all. The reason for this is it gains strength based on a person's thoughts. Fear on its own doesn't have any power. Power is given to it based on how we act in the face of it. Power is given to it because it is never overcome when you try to simply tuck it away. Imagined fears have kept so many people from reaching their full potential. Fear is the weed in your mind that is starving all of your drive. It is suffocating your initiative and stifling your action. You must develop the courage needed to face that fear.

Franklin D. Roosevelt once said, "Courage isn't the absence of fear, but rather the assessment that something else is more important that fear." What's more important than your fear of failure?

Fear of embarrassment?

Fear of the unknown?

I'll tell you what's more important: the vision you have for your future. The goals you have set for yourself. Rising up in the face of fear and walking in your purpose.

Imagined fear creates a narrative that has to be managed lest it will strangle the life out of everything you aim to become. You must face it head-on. Your ability to face fear doesn't just build character, it reveals character.

The pleasure principle put forth by Sigmund Freud describes how we will do anything to let us avoid pain and move us closer to pleasure. Fear for many people is a mental pain that we would rather steer away from. So instead of facing it head-on, we look for other things that can give us a pleasurable feeling.

There are also fear triggers. One of the greatest of all is the fear of darkness or the loss of visibility, not being able to see your surroundings. Children are terrified of the dark because of monsters they have created in their minds. Adults do the same thing. When it is dark you cannot see what is in front of you, all of your other senses are heightened and every sound, smell, and sensation you feel becomes amplified. You become more careful of each step and you are hesitant to move without caution. All you need is a little light to help you face the fear. Everything changes when there is a little light. When there is light, you're willing to walk further than you would without it. You're willing to move further away from the comforts of the campsite because you can see.

Nelson Mandela said, "I learned that courage was not the absence of fear, but the triumph over it. The brave man is not he who does not feel afraid, but he who conquers fear."

Let your goals and your dreams be the light in the darkness that you depend on.

How do you get rid of fear? By shedding some light on it. Here are a couple strategies you can try:

1. Repeated Exposure

When there is a regular occurrence of the things that cause fear, it leads to familiarity which reduces fear and the response we have to it. Each occurrence reduces the power, bit by bit, of what causes the fear itself. For example, if someone was afraid of spiders, there would be a progressive approach to help them work on their fear. The first thing wouldn't be holding a tarantula. The first thing could be having a conversation about it. Then it could be seeing a photo of one. After seeing the picture, the next step could be watching a video. Once the person has been exposed and grown accustomed to all of those, you can allow them to see a real spider in a glass tank. This process goes on, moving by degrees, so that you can face those fears and get things back in your control. What does the process look like for you?

2. Starve It of Its Power

Don't believe the curse. Don't allow anything anyone has said to you or spoken over your life to take control. I do not care who told you what you wanted to do was impossible. The only thing that is impossible is the thing that you won't try. Don't be fearful, be fearless. Be fearless in the face of uncertainty. Be fearless when the future doesn't seem bright. So what if you can't see it? People feel themselves getting sick before it takes over. You can feel the atmosphere change before the storm arrives. You have the feeling first before it gets there. Therefore, the feeling you have for your purpose, the feeling you have for your greatness, is a glimpse of what is sure to come once you decide to make a change.

"You block your dream when you allow your fear to grow bigger than your faith." —Mary Manin Morrissey

48

Be a Beast, But First...

O NE THING I love is listening to motivational speeches. They get me excited. They make me want to be a better person right away. The stories of success all serve as an example of what you can achieve. One of my favorite speeches to listen to talks about becoming a beast. The mentality of a beast is different. The way they hunt is different. The way they move is different. But there are things that must happen before you can be a beast. No amount of motivation, guts, or pride can make up for lack of preparation. You can be as excited as you want to be, but when you are met with the real world and you are met with real life circumstances that challenge your inner being, if you are not prepared you will fail. It is important to understand that to operate at a higher level, there are things you need to do first. If you are not mentally ready for battle, how can you possibly think you will win the war? Be a beast, but first take care of your mind.

The only way to become a beast is if you take care of all the internal things that prevented you from becoming a beast in the first place. Some people have internal issues with self-esteem and self-worth that they must deal with first before they can tackle the big things and enter beast mode. Once they address those issues and start believing in themselves, they can become that person who attacks everything with vigor and tenacity. But until then, it's not possible. The problem is people get so motivated and inspired in the moment after hearing motivational speeches or slogans like "be the beast" that they neglect to do the less glamorous (but important) things that need to be done first before going out to accomplish the things they said they wanted to do. If you don't manage the issues that are happening internally, you risk allowing those simple things to destroy the beast. They become the thorn in your side. Your Achilles heel.

I like to relate it to fruit and how fast it can be ruined just by one spot of mold. Once one part goes bad, the rest of the fruit starts developing the same fungus making the whole thing deteriorate. And it started with the small things. It is the small things that start to eat away at the moral fabric of who you want to be. It is the small things that start to take away your desire to become what you need to be. It is the small things that prevent you from seeing what you need to see. It is the small things that start to make your goals more distant and cause you to go back and forth and wayward in your decision making. In order to be a beast, you must take care of the small things. Start working from the inside out.

49

The Mariana Trench

A T 36,201 FEET sits the Challenger Deep, located in the Mariana Trench, the deepest point in Earth's ocean floor. It is said that if you were to take Mount Everest and place it there, the mountain's peak would still be covered by more than a mile of water. The first measurement of the trench's depth was taken by the British in 1875 and was determined to be 26,850 feet. Then in 1951, another Royal Navy vessel measured it at 35,760 feet. The reason these discoveries are important is that each time they searched, they went deeper. The deeper they went, the more species of animal and other organisms they found, as well as new means of exploring the deep.

The exploration into the depths of the Mariana Trench is yet another natural reminder of what we need to do within ourselves. How deeply we dive into our hearts and minds are truly only relative to where we are in life at the time and our ability to understand and make sense of what's there. As we mature in our walk, we are better suited to take a deeper dive.

When explorers first journeyed into the ocean depth, they didn't have the equipment to go further than they did. Likewise, many of us aren't equipped with the tools or the experience and mentally and physically speaking, aren't prepared to handle the pressure that comes from going that deep. Earlier, we talked about how being on the potter's wheel would force you to dig up some things you may want to keep buried. As you continue on your journey and dig deeper, you'll uncover those things, and some of those things, just like the creatures that live in the depths, are terrifying and will make you face your worst troubles and fears. What you do in those times will determine your success and speak to your destiny.

50

Deep Scan

IN ORDER TO elevate, it is important that you do a deep self-scan. Consider the following story:

After tweaking his knee, Mark found himself dealing with a nagging injury that prevented him from being able to play the game he loved most. He was good at what he did. He knew his position so well that no matter the situation or the problem the other team presented, he was ready to beat it. After repeated attempts to play with the injury, things continued to get worse. Finally, his coach was able to get him to go in for an MRI. After arriving, he lies down and his knee is placed in a brace to minimize movement. He was told to stay as still as possible so that the images will come out clearly. But Mark just couldn't keep still, and what should've taken twenty minutes ended up being more than an hour. Finally the MRI was complete and he was free to go. Before he left, the doctor said, "Hey I know you don't want to be here but this is what it takes if you want to get to the next level. Nothing else is more important than figuring out what the injury is so it can be treated. I knew there were many different things that were going on in your mind in there. Thoughts about your future, the game, and how long it would take to heal, but there are many life lessons to be learned by getting an MRI." He explained that the MRI helps doctors to find the problem and more importantly, identify the root cause of it so they can put together the best treatment plan to help him recover. Mark's job was to hold still for as long as possible so that the clearest images could be taken and they could determine steps for future healing.

In life, sometimes you are going to have to slow down and sit still to find out who you really are so that the plan for your future can be clearly seen. Although you may not be comfortable and you might feel locked in place, being stuck in that position forces you to focus on what is happening in the moment and to find yourself.

There are so many examples to follow all around us. Not everyone is meant to be like Oprah. Not everyone's calling is to be Brené Brown. What you can do along your journey of discovering who you are is think of the great influences you may have had and take some of those things and make them a part of your journey's DNA. You can be an actress and make the same impacts on the screen as Viola Davis without trying to be her. You must follow the beat of your own drum and follow the path that others have paved for you. And if you must deviate from that path to go in the direction of self-discovery, then go.

By doing this, you will uncover what your strengths are, what your weaknesses are, and areas that you might not have even recognized.

I took three personality tests in the last few years. The first one I took was the DISC personality test. The second test I took was similar, except this one was at church and it told me my ministry leadership style. The third one I took was a personality test at a leadership academy. All three of these tests told me the same thing. They told me that I am truly driven by success. It highlighted the fact that I enjoy empowering people and that their overall health and success mattered to me. It said I love being the life of a party, and it said I was emotional and sensitive. All of the first facts I agree with, but I completely disagree with that last part. Okay, I'm kidding, but during my deep scan of finding myself and identifying who I was, I realized I was indeed emotional....and sensitive.

On the surface, hearing that stung a bit because of the associations I had with those words and what they meant to me growing up. Sensitive meant soft. Emotional meant you were a crybaby. Although I view these words as positive things now, it took some time for to get there because of what emotions I had attached to them. We have to be careful what emotions and characteristics we attach to certain words because they have the power to shape people. Maybe as a woman you have been told being sensitive isn't a good thing in the workplace, so you feel you need to put on a tougher face to be respected. Although you may get the job done, you may also be seen as mean and unapproachable.

The purpose of the deep scan is to find who you really are and develop your strengths as you head towards purpose and fulfillment.

To my children and to everyone reading this: You are who you are. You are uniquely you. Feel what you feel. You are created by the creator, designed by the designer, and molded by the molder.

"Be yourself; everyone else is already taken." —Oscar Wilde

51

Extreme Ownership

YOU ARE WHERE you are today because of the things you have done and the things you have not done up to this point in life. There is no other way to put it. Your position today represents the sum of all your efforts and, whether good or bad, where you stand today reading this (mentally, physically, emotionally, spiritually) is your pin on the map. The beautiful part about this is that you have the opportunity to move that pin. In order to move it, there is a mental action step that needs to take place.

What I'd like for you to do from this point on is recognize this and understand that the key to being able to move forward, in a way that doesn't put you back in that same place, is to take ownership of where you are today. For years I have wanted to become more flexible. I have always been athletic in some way but the ability to be *bendy* is something I have always desired. In addition to that desire, a good friend of mine who is a physical therapist told me I was extremely *tight* and that if I wanted to be able to maintain my active lifestyle injury free and be able to play with my grandkids, I'd have to put more effort into stretching. So what did I do? I said I would give it a solid effort and make stretching a daily practice. I went and bought yoga blocks, stretching mats, assisting straps, I mean the whole yogi starter kit. The only thing I was missing was some lavender. Well, I'll let you in on my little secret: I am still not flexible, and it is not because of anything other than me not making it a priority. Since I didn't move stretching up higher on my priority list, I must now own where I am today. And where is that? There are a few more cracks and pops when I first get going in the morning, and my recovery after tough workouts…let's just say they take a little longer than usual. If we look at the end result, it was my responsibility. I didn't hold myself accountable and now I must own it.

Responsibility + Accountability = Ownership

Ownership looks different based on where a person is in life. The CEO of a company, a high school teacher, an accountant, and an entrepreneur all have different job descriptions, yet to be successful, they all require a certain level of ownership.

Fill in the gaps

Extreme ownership means taking everything that comes with the good as well as what comes with the bad. It means owning the A you made after studying all week as well as owning the F you got when you chose to party it up instead. It means taking the kids to practice on time and owning when you worked later than you should have and arrived ten minutes late. Extreme ownership makes it impossible for you to point the finger in another direction and forces you to accept that you didn't do what you said you would do.

There are many things that prevent extreme ownership. It could be that you make too many excuses. You may see everyone else as the reason why you aren't where you want to be. Lastly, you haven't made it a priority. How can you remedy this?

1. Recognize your role in where you are.

2. Look at the errors and work diligently at fixing them.

3. Stop worrying about what others may think.

52

Priorities

P   I   R   T   E

R   O   I   I   S

OUR PRIORITIES AREN'T in line. When we know we should focus on a task, it seems like we always find something else to do.

Have you ever had a night when you weren't able to sleep? Did you lay there and watch the time tick away on the clock telling yourself that if you just laid there a few more minutes you would eventually fall asleep? I know I've personally done that on many occasions. For me there were just so many things going on in my head. All of my thoughts were centered around things I wanted to accomplish. They were all business ideas and book titles. Even poetry at times. But I would lay there for hours on end, never deciding to just get up and make the most out of having breath in my body. Even though I had the thought. Even though I had the ability to just do something. I didn't do it. Why? It was simply not important enough. Sleep was more important. Or at least the desire to sleep. I began to see rather quickly that I valued resting more than I did working towards something that would eventually afford me the opportunity to rest as much as I wanted. Rest was my priority.

The thing about priorities is that they change daily. They change continuously because we are humans, and this is real life, and in real life plans will change. Here's an example. It's time for you to go to work, so you get up and start to go through your normal routine. You freshen up, you get dressed, you grab your already made self-timed coffee (because coffee will always be priority), you stuff your lunch in your bag and head out the door. On the way to work, you are quickly reminded by the beeping sound coupled with your gas light blinking on of how you ignored it last night. Now the decision making process has to happen again. This decision is going to be made based on a new set of priorities. You know you can't be late, but you know you need gas. Not only does this scenario force you to establish new priorities, it forces you to look at your earlier actions (or lack thereof) and prompts an immediate self-assessment. You probably should have stopped for gas on your way home last night, knowing it would only make you late this morning. But does this mean you'll never make that same decision again? Many times that self-assessment is acknowledged then ignored. When you look at that assessment and work towards preventing it from happening again, you restructure your priorities. When you ignore it, you allow the same pattern to continue. If you refuse to change your viewpoint, you'll continue to do the same thing.

53

Make the U-turn

HAVE YOU EVER been sitting at home or driving around and all of a sudden been hit by a crazy craving for something specific? That sandwich you love from that restaurant or an ice cream from that spot in town?

What do you do when that happens? You load the family up and you head there. And if you're driving in the opposite direction, you will make a U-turn. You'll cut off an old lady in traffic. You'll do anything just to get to that spicy chicken deluxe with a chocolate shake. (That's not me, y'all, this part is about my bride.)

But it feels good when you get there and you order the food and they hit you with that "My pleasure" as you pull away from the pick-up window. It is so satisfying when you finally get to eat the thing you've been craving. Sometimes you don't even get out of the drive-through before your hand is on a waffle fry.

It feels good to get it, right?

It feels good to want something, turn around to go get it, and get it right away.

It would be amazing if that could happen with everything in life, wouldn't it? If we wanted something at the moment and let nothing stand in the way of us getting it. Even if it takes you off course, making the detour to get to what you want most will be worth it. It is about reminding yourself of that desire. It is about being hungry again and having a thirst for excellence.

At some point in your life, you had the desire to do something, become something, or go somewhere. Some of you even attempted to do it and sometimes you accomplished it, other times you didn't. Every one of you reading this has something inside of you that you want to achieve. However, just because you have the desire to do something doesn't mean it is going to happen. It won't be as simple as making a U-turn and hitting the drive-through.

But the U-turn itself just might be necessary, because if you are still traveling down the same roads, doing the same things, talking to and trusting and believing in the same people who have kept you on that same path you've been on for years, the end result is going to be the same.

Not everyone in your life is meant to be there for every season. Sometimes separation needs to happen. You may have to cut some people off. Admittedly, there have been times when I may have "accidentally cut some people off on purpose" in traffic. But it was necessary because if I didn't make that turn, I was going to end up so far off course that it would take me another fifteen minutes to get back on track. Now, in no way am I encouraging erratic driving. What I am saying is you need to take charge of the wheel and be willing to change directions to accomplish the mission. You need to be willing to take a detour to get away from some things, people, and environments that are holding you back. And you have to do it with a sense of urgency.

54

Your Hourglass Has Been Tipped

URGENCY: THE QUALITY of state of being compelling or requiring immediate action or attention; dire; pressing

I hate to be the one to tell you this, but you aren't going to be here forever, and it is time to move and operate with a sense of urgency. Your hourglass has already been tipped and the sand has already begun to drain. You don't know if there is more sand on the top or bottom right now, but if there is one thing you can be sure of, it is that time will eventually run out. Knowing this to be true, what are you waiting for? What is it going to take for you to take action and start living the purpose-driven life that will finally bring you the fulfillment you have been longing for? If you're looking for permission to start, not that you need it but, **permission granted**.

Many people are allowing themselves to waste precious moments of their lives hiding in the safety and security of their jobs. We are too fearful of what may happen if we don't succeed. We care more about what someone else would think about us than we do ourselves. No one else has to look in the mirror and face the person you face every day but you. Just as no one else will be able to do what you have been created to do. There is a gift in you that you need to share with the world.

It may be that you're a speaker and you are passionate about women advocacy because of the things you've gone through in your life. You may be a veteran searching to find your place in the world, but it may be your job to create it. No matter who you are, you have a story to tell because of the things you've endured. A story that has the potential to pull someone into the light. A story that can make someone decide "I am worth it" and "I can achieve greatness." You may be the researcher who has spent countless hours on your dissertation but hasn't taken the next step to defend it, but what you have to say might be the breakthrough that the world needs to solve the issue with sustainable energy. Your message belongs on a stage. Your voice belongs on the radio. Your story belongs in a book.

The hourglass has been tipped and you don't know how much time you have left before those stories have to go with you. You may be an artist who has a room full of completed works that are collecting dust yet should be on someone's mantle. Or in a museum. You're the gifted graphic designer, poet, dancer, musician, teacher, entrepreneur, designer, preacher who has something else that no one else has, so I am giving you the permission to go and be great. There is no time to wait.

On the journey towards purpose and fulfillment, you will need to identify what your natural gifts, talents, and abilities are. Many of you may be confused on what direction you are supposed to go in life and that is because you haven't identified what it is that lights your fire. Your purpose isn't going to be found by going to Google and typing in "top fulfilling jobs to find my purpose." You also won't be able to get to it if your environment isn't conducive to what it takes to get to your goals. So what is it you want to do?

Do you love research?

Do you love helping people?

Do you dream of owning a business?

Is your dream to be a doctor or a pilot? Maybe real estate or custom work is your thing. No matter what it is you want to do, in order to elevate, you need to work at it tirelessly and be so good at it that the world can't ignore you.

Seneca said, "You live as if you were destined to live forever, no thought of your frailty ever enters your head, of how much time has already gone by. You take no heed. You squander time as if you drew from a full and abundant supply, though all the while that day which you bestow on some person or thing is perhaps your last."

We aren't blessed with immortality but our messages can be. Simon Sinek speaks of finite versus infinite things. Things that are finite have a beginning, middle, and end. We know that we are born, we will live, and eventually, we will pass on, but what will we make of this life? What will we make of the time that we have here to be able to say in the end "I am satisfied," and "I am fulfilled"? Personally, I desire to live an infinite life. Sinek says, the infinite life is the one where the things you have done, the words you have said, the actions you have taken will continue to echo throughout ages to come. The finite and the infinite life have consequences. What you choose to do has the potential to be transformational in people's minds and lives, and what you refuse to do must be done by someone else.

Think about what would've happened if Rosa Parks didn't sit and if Martin Luther King Jr. didn't dream. What if Neil Armstrong never journeyed to the moon? What if Albert Einstein quit on the ninety-ninth attempt? What would have become of Beethoven, Gandhi, Mandela, and countless others if they did none of the things they are now known for? All these people did things that have left a mark on humanity and there are millions of others who could have and did not. Where will you be placed at the end of your time? Will your works be spoken of after you're gone? Will you be remembered? If our hourglasses have already been tipped, then it is time to start taking risks, stop fearing rejection, and get to the water.

55

Get To The Water

BURIED ALMOST TWO feet under the sand, a hundred ping-pong-ball-sized eggs have been incubating for roughly sixty days. With the use of hydrophones, researchers can hear the sounds of the baby sea turtles preparing to make their grand entrance into the world. As they reach the surface, crowds of onlookers stare in amazement as the two-inch long turtles make their way to the ocean to begin a life cycle that has been the source of aquatic exploration for many years. This will be the last time many of these turtles will be seen by humans. Some will not survive and there will be others who become giants in the sea.

Imagine being born, having to dig your way out of wet sand, and right away having to sprint a hundred-meter dash, knowing that there are dangers awaiting you and that you are defenseless, but you still must make the trip. A trip that requires you to face adversity and fight for survival before you even have a chance to draw your first breaths.

Some of you don't have to imagine that at all because that's your story. Your life hasn't been easy and things haven't been handed to you. For some of you, the broken home you grew up in caused you to have to endure physical, mental, and emotional abuse. Maybe the divorce derailed your plans in life and having to start over felt like you were digging your way out from under the weight of so much wet sand. Maybe because of the absence of your father you didn't learn the things you needed to learn so you sought out lessons elsewhere and the things you learned instead have hindered you. Perhaps you were abandoned and the time in and out of foster care made you feel as if no one cared. If any of this is true for you, or you have a story of adversity that has held you back, then it is time to break out.

Baby sea turtles are born with a temporary egg tooth called a caruncle. No, this isn't biology class, but this is important to understand. They use that tooth to break out of the shell and immediately get to work. They don't know why they are doing what they are doing, they simply feel compelled to crawl their way out of the sand and to head toward the brightest horizon. There is something in their genetic makeup that says to them, "Break out, claw your way to the surface, and get to the water." Your caruncle is any tool that motivates you. Use your goals as your caruncle. Let your purpose be the thing that breaks you out of your shell.

Breaking out of your shell means shaking off that thing that's holding you back (your yoke, your chains, your addiction, your shackles) and getting to the water (your dreams, your goals, your aspirations, your purpose) like your life depends on it, because it does.

Here's something incredible: there was a study done at the University of Western Sydney in 2011 that found that certain species of turtle had the ability to communicate with other turtles in the embryonic stage to let them know that it was nearing the time to hatch. This communication prompted the less developed turtles to increase their growth rate so they could all hatch around the same time. Well, listen up. It's time. I know you may not think you're ready. You may be scared and you may feel unprepared. There is a world of predators lying in wait for you, but you don't have to worry about that because we are going to move together. I know you are still developing, but it is time to get going. I know the journey is going to be hard, but it is going to be worth it. How do I know? Because I have been there and I am trying to show you the way. The path is the hardest for the first one who ventures forth. That first turtle is moving on instinct. That second one has instinct and a path. All of you have example after example of what hard work looks like. Examples of what success looks like. The path has already been created. I just need you to break out, claw your way to the surface, get to the water and get lost.

56

Get Lost

IMAGINE THIS, IF you will: Long before the days of Waze, Google Maps, Apple Maps, and MapQuest, there was an ancient tool called a map. This tool was used to navigate oceans far and wide, traverse battlefields, and even guided gold hunters out West. The purpose of the map was to help travelers get from point A to point B, and it did, unless it was in the wrong hands. Many drivers have found themselves hours off course on a road trip after trusting the passenger with the map. Speaking of getting to the water, there are stories of people who have followed their GPSs right to it.

With or without the maps of old or modern GPS systems, we have still found ourselves lost at some point in time. But being lost isn't always a bad thing. I have stumbled across some of the best places to eat, taken the best photos, and relaxed, all while being lost. I learned to appreciate what I had because in that moment, I wanted nothing more than to find my way back home, and when I did, I was able to appreciate the time I spent being lost and I was able to learn from it.

The Sargasso Sea is where many of those little hatchlings would find themselves and where they would dwell to feed and grow. From the time the turtles take their first swim to when they return to coastal waters to forage as juveniles, more than a decade may have passed. This period of time is often referred to as the "lost years" since following sea turtles' movements during this phase is difficult and their whereabouts are often unknown. The female turtles are known to come back to the same beaches where they were born some fifteen to twenty years later to lay their eggs. Scientists have been baffled as to how this happens but now understand that each coastline has a unique magnetic signature and through what is known as geomagnetic imprinting, turtles can navigate their way back to their natal beach to lay their eggs despite spending years away.

What happened during the time when they were away isn't well known, but what is known is that they were able to navigate troubled waters, nurture themselves, weather storm after storm, and return to give birth.

It's time to get lost.

As a matter of fact, I dare you to get lost.

People usually don't want to get lost because that means being alone. Being alone forces you to face yourself and every challenge that comes your way without depending on others. We don't want to get lost because too much time away means we may miss out on something. You're scared of being tossed by the sea of your fears. You're afraid of what it might expose in you. You're scared to be vulnerable.

But it's time to get lost.

Get lost and don't come back until you're ready. There is danger in coming back home before you're prepared. When you aren't fully developed, mentally and emotionally, it is easy to fall back into the same patterns, and you can't allow that to happen. You need to get to your personal Sargasso Sea and spend some time there alone. When was the last time you were alone? I don't mean simply being by yourself. You can be by yourself and still not be alone. When was the last time you were by yourself, not working on a task, not on your cell phone, not watching TV or listening to a podcast? When was the last time you were alone with just you and your thoughts? For many of you, the answer might be never, but time alone is necessary. Being lost can lead to self-discovery.

Being lost will not only build character but it will also reveal character. It shows you what you're made of. Getting lost is about self-awareness and using that awareness to create change within you.

It is in those quiet moments with no one and nothing but yourself that you will find out who you really are. That isolation will give you the freedom and peace that you need. It is time for you to get lost. During that time away, you will become harder. Solitude is where you will find solace. It is where you will find your strength. When you're lost, you can only think about what's most important to you at that moment and that is finding yourself first. Only after you find yourself and develop into who you are called to be can the journey back home begin. The difference this time, now that you are ready, is that you will be ready to bring forth every new idea, that which will take you from finite to infinite.

It is okay to be apprehensive. It is okay to ask questions. It is not okay to do nothing. You've already made it to the water, so get ahead. Get lost.

57

The Other Side of Lost

SOME OF YOU have been feeling lost for a long time. You might be lost for a multitude of reasons. Some of you are lost because you lost someone close to you. Others are lost because someone you loved hurt you and you haven't been able to move forward. Some of you are lost because you're not happy with a relationship or with your current job situation.

It's okay to feel lost. It's okay to be alone sometimes. As a matter of fact, you need to be alone because many times the situations you found yourself in could have been avoided had you intentionally gotten lost. The difference in some of our situations is that you've been trying to be found.

Now is the time for you to embrace your lost years. You need to yearn for the lost years because this is the time when you have the opportunity to grow.

We can't always depend on others. The sea turtles are only together long enough to get to the water. They don't stay together forever, and neither should we. The good book tells us there is a time and a season for everything. From that initial hatching call to hitting the water is the amount of time the turtles get together. After that, life takes them their separate ways.

Some of you have tried to take everyone with you and that is the reason you haven't progressed as much. Some of you have been taking mental baggage with you and it's slowing you down.

Get to the water and get lost. Getting lost means you will be alone, you will feel like an outcast, you will be judged, labeled, and misunderstood.

But if you can continue to run this race despite all of these things standing against you, if you can embrace the hardship and make it through this time in your life, I promise you, success is going to feel like you never thought it would feel. Success is going to taste like you never thought it would taste. It is going to be the best thing that you've ever had.

58

Break Out The Yellow Tape

I N ORDER TO get to where you are supposed to go and become who you are supposed to be, there are changes that must be made. Many of you reading this may need to start all over because your foundation has been built on the wrong ground. Because of the things you've gone through, many of the walls of your mind need to be remodeled and there are others that need to be broken down all together.

There are some things you will be able to keep but there are other things in your mind that need to be gutted. Some of you have gone off course because you have allowed mental squatters to take up residence and their presence is no longer welcome. An eviction notice for anything not contibuting to you being the best version of you must be served. It is time to put the world on notice and it is time to break out the yellow tape. You must cordon and block off your personal space to go under construction because there are areas in your life that need improvement. Breaking out the yellow tape is necessary to elevate because elevation requires change. In order for you to find and walk in your purpose, you must constantly be willing to go under construction.

What are the areas in your life that need to be improved? Is there doubt that needs to be demolished? Are you holding on to hurt from the past that prevents you from being renewed? Are you dealing with grief from loss? Is it a mental health issue that you continue to place on the backburner?

Many construction sites use scaffolding to hide what's being built underneath. Some of you need to put up some scaffolding and mark a construction zone because what you are working on isn't meant to be seen by everyone else. It is just about you. This is your time to look inward at your life, get off social media, and get rid of the things that are holding you back.

Breaking out the yellow tape and going under construction is critical so you can address some of the foundational issues that have plagued you your entire life. There may be some childhood trauma that you've held on to that has prevented you from going forward. Going under construction means breaking through walls of hurt, anger, and pain so you can address the issue and get rid of it. Get rid of everything that doesn't belong there. The longer you allow it to live inside of you, the more it eats away at who you are destined to be.

Some of you have never been able to move on after dealing with the loss of a close friend or loved one. Where there was once joy and hope, now there is only sorrow and grief. Putting the pieces together after your loss might be the hardest thing you've ever attempted to do. In this phase of construction in your life, you don't have to forget them, but you do have to live for them. You have to be the beacon of light for yourself first and foremost, and secondly, for everyone who sees you as their lighthouse.

Perhaps your inability to forgive someone who has hurt you has been a barrier to you rebuilding. Someone abandoned you and because of that it has been hard for you to give of yourself freely and difficult for you to trust. I am here to tell you that in order for you to be free, made new, and elevate, you are going to have to break out your yellow tape and go under construction. You can't allow the tragedies you've been through to keep you mentally bound.

Yes, this means you will have to draw away from society for a bit. Yes, it means you will have to address what is happening inside. Yes, it will be difficult, and no, it will not be pretty. It means accepting that some things will need to be demolished, hauled away, and reconstructed.

Going under construction means acknowledging that you don't know everything, but you do have the will to learn. Time is up for just covering the walls with a fresh coat of paint. It is time to break out the yellow tape and it is time to put on the hard hat so you can get to work.

59

One Action Step

IF EVERYTHING YOU wanted was just one step away, how willing would you be to take that step? I'd venture to say that you would not hesitate at all. You would run! What I am asking you to do is to get ready to do that. I want you to identify what it is you want. I don't care if it's ten different things. Write them all out. Put it on paper so you can see it. Gone are the days of allowing great thoughts to be lost in the mix of our daily lives. Identify everything you're interested in and from there, you can start narrowing it down. Don't be deterred by people on the outside telling you what they think you should do. There are a lot of dreams that lie dormant because someone chose to follow the path their parents chose for them and not the path they wanted for themselves. You are one action step away from your break though.

Les Brown said, "The graveyard is the richest place on earth, because it is here that you will find all the hopes and dreams that were never fulfilled, the books that were never written, the songs that were never sung, the inventions that were never shared, the cures that were never discovered, all because someone was too afraid to take that first step." I refuse to allow that to be my story and you're reading this because it won't be yours.

It doesn't matter to me if you haven't figured life out yet. I mean, I'm still trying to figure out what I want to be when I grow up, but I am driven to get there. I don't write this book as someone who has it all figured out. I write this book because I am you. I am the person who needed to find the drive to start and develop the motivation and the discipline to finish. I am the person who started multiple times. I am the guy that changed his major in college more than once, but guess what? It's my story and I am the creator. As long as I have breath in my body, I can continue to press towards the mark. The key is positioning yourself to start. You can never win a race if you never get to the starting blocks. I don't care if you're in prison or trying to be the next president. Every one of us is only one step away from changing our lives for the better.

60

Elevation Requires Action

CHANGING A BEHAVIOR starts with recognizing what you were doing was not conducive to the desired end result. It means creating new neural pathways by being consistent and intentional in your actions. You must become conscious of each step you take. You have to be grateful and you have to appreciate the journey. Be thankful for all the things you were able to do. Don't beat yourself up over a setback. You're a human being, and as humans, we make mistakes. It is impossible to start something new and do it without error a hundred percent of the time. If that were possible, then all of us would be professional athletes, doctors, CEOs, scholars, and rocket scientists. But we're not. Those people made it to that point because of total dedication to their craft and their desires. Therefore, forming healthy habits was key for them in reaching their goals. Countless hours of studying and innumerable more of practical application, all to get to a degree, all to get to their goal. You will never get the call you desire if you don't master the skill of creating healthy habits.

Get Away

One action step you may need to take is to get away. Your current surroundings may be holding you in place. I know so many people who have the potential to change their lives if only they had the courage to get up and leave their current situations. Most of them don't and because of it they suffer.

As the weather changes toward colder temperatures, animals all over the world start preparing for the transition. Bears gorge themselves with food because the hibernation period will be long, and they will need nourishment. Other animals migrate to other regions where the weather is more temperate for better living conditions and for reproductive needs. The migration is essential for their survival. It is an action step that is necessary for them and it is one that is necessary for you. It is time to get away. Getting away will allow you to gain new focus and will bring clarity to your mind as to what tomorrow should look like for you. But first, you have to make the decision to move.

61

Decision Making

EVERY DAY WE must make decisions. We have to decide what we want to wear for the day, what we want to eat for the day, what time we have to leave to go to work….the day is full of decisions. Some of the decisions we make are ones that don't require much thought, and then there are other decisions that we have to be a bit more focused on.

Deciding whether you want your sandwich on white bread or wheat isn't as complex as submitting a report on time to your boss. One requires you to put time and effort into it to ensure the accuracy and thoroughness of that report, the other just requires….a decision. Not every decision we make will be good. Sometimes we make decisions and they end up being bad ones. We make bad career choices. We choose bad relationships.

All decisions we make have consequences. Consequences aren't always bad. A consequence is the result of your behavior. If you put forth effort in studying, the consequence of that action should be a good grade. If you didn't fill up the tank because you thought there would be cheaper gas at the next exit, the consequence of that could be running out of gas (I know this firsthand).

There are other times the decisions that you make will have ripple effect throughout the rest of your life. If you've ever skipped a rock over the water, at the moment of impact, the ripple starts. The more force behind the rock, the bigger the ripples in the water. For the big decisions you make in life, the ripple effect or the consequences, will go on much longer and will have a greater impact.

When I made the decision to transition out of the Marine Corps, it was a decision that I knew would have many aftereffects; however, I knew it was a decision I had to make. My future depended on it, and the happiness of my heart hinged upon it. I knew if I didn't act on what I knew I needed to do, that I would be putting off my vision. Tomorrow isn't promised to any of us so I was no longer willing to take that chance. I believed in me.

I will admit that I feel I was better prepared than most people would likely be to make a major decision like that. From the moment recruit training starts, recruits in their quest to become Marines are taught to believe in themselves. They are taught to be different. They are taught to take chances. They are taught to face adversity head on. For me, this was just an amplified version of the way I was raised. There is no doubt that stepping away from the military was difficult. Two years prior to me actually doing it, I decided I would stay a little longer. It wasn't easy, especially with an organization like the Marine Corps. It doesn't matter what field you're in, walking away from something that you have been doing for over twenty years isn't easy even if it had to be done. I had to trust that the ripple effect that would affect me and my family's way of life would be worth it.

The question now is when it comes to your dreams, is it worth it to you? Yes, it will affect your comfort level. Yes, it means you might have some hard times. Yes, others will view you differently but if you're truly following what you think is your calling, and if you are the person you say you are, you have to make that decision regardless of what the consequences might look like. Just know that everything is going to work out for your good.

The Latin origin of the word decide is *decidere*, which is made up of two parts: *de*, meaning "off," and *caedere*, meaning "to cut." If we were to look at the origin of this word, then to decide means to cut something off. To decide means to cut off all other options, to remove some things out of your life. It is the pruning of the plant that causes it to continue to grow and bloom. You must cut the dead things away so that growth can be stimulated. Prune what is no longer purposeful. Be confident in your decision.

> When it is time to make a decision, "first say to yourself what you would be, and then do what you have to do." – Epictetus

Deciding to make a change will be difficult because everything has a consequence. The consequences shouldn't stop you from making the decision, they should just serve their place in influencing it. What play do you call when it's fourth down and the game is on the line? Do you run the ball or do you pass? Do you kick a field goal now or should you try to get a little closer? When troops are in contact with the enemy and they are being overrun, they need immediate air support. You understand that dropping rounds when the enemy is close means you may injure or even kill a fellow comrade. Is it worth taking the chance if it could completely neutralize the enemy and all your men and women make it home safely?

When Zarifa Ghafari received a letter from the Taliban telling her she would be assassinated if she continued pushing for girls to be educated, she could have decided to go silent. When she was told to step down from her position as mayor, she could have walked away. Instead of facing the pain of regret by bowing to the pressures of a formidable enemy, she decided she would continue on regardless of the risks because she was following her purpose.

When you're trying to figure out what it is you're supposed to be doing, it can be increasingly difficult. When someone is driven by their purpose and their passion, decision making is easy.

62

The Hunt

HUNTING IS NO different for humans than it is for animals. You are going to come back empty handed far more often than you will come back with a prize buck. Despite this reality, if you want to eat, if you want to feed your family, you still have to go back out the next day and hunt again. The ability to get up and head out the door again, the will to pack the pack again, to load the rifle again, to sit in the stand again, determines whether or not you and your family are going to eat. A lion can't just say, "Well, I've gone out twice and I didn't find anything so there must be nothing to eat." The lioness can't say, "I've gone out twice, I've gone out three times, I've gone out for the last two weeks and I haven't found food and so I quit." She can't quit because she has cubs to feed.

You can't go another day without filling out another job application just because you haven't been called in for an interview after the first ten. You have to be active in the hunt. You have to show you want it. You have to be the one to put yourself out there, call them back, and make them see that you want that position. Too many times pride gets in the way and people can't bring themselves to go back and fill out another application. Well, pride comes before the fall and, in the case of lions, pride can kill a pride. This means your decisions or lack of decisions affect more than you. You have to go on another interview, you have to go and do another sales presentation, you have to go into another casting call, you have to do whatever you need to do again and again until the hunt is successful.

Tom Brady is a great example of someone who believed in the hunt. He went from being a sixth round draft pick to the greatest of all time. You don't get to that point without being driven and without having the will to work hard day in and day out. He knew he needed to eat (win) which meant he needed to get up every single day and hunt. Nobody else saw what he'd become, but I would bet my life that he knew what he would become.

Your ability to go back out again after coming home empty handed is a factor of how badly you want it. How bad do you want that goal you have set your mind to, and are you willing to prove it? It's not about proving it to anyone else either. So many people get caught up in trying to please other people and telling others their goals that it prevents them from actually making progress toward what they said they wanted. The only people you should be talking to about your hunt should be those who are on the hunt with you. Those who are contributing to your success and those who want to see you succeed. Not those who just want to be in it for the thrill. You need people in your corner who are actively hunting themselves. Hunting takes patience and if they're not on the hunt with you, they won't be able to understand why it means so much to you. Hunting means planning, preparation, being proactive, and being comfortable with sitting in silence so you can see the opportunity when it presents itself.

The Silent Hunter

Everyone doesn't need to know what you're doing. Stop wasting your time seeking validation for the idea and put in the work. I can say this because I've been that person. The more I talked about the thing I wanted to do, the better it made me feel. As long as I had a nice sounding idea, I felt that was enough. But in the end, it was all talk. I was only fooling myself. You can only pull the wool over your own eyes for so long before reality hits you.

Have you ever played the word game where you take the letters from one word and see how many other words you can make out of those letters? It's no mistake that the words silent and listen are made from the same letters.

You can't hear what you need to take in if you aren't silent. Talking about the hunt does nothing, but when you can sit in silence, your ability to hear what you long for becomes heightened.

When you sit in silence for the first time it can be uncomfortable. You may become bored. But as you continue to do it, you'll soon begin to realize that silence is louder than you expected.

Hunting Means Waking Up Early

To be able to be successful on a hunt, you have to get up early. Being up early allows you to get into the right position before the animal you're trying to hunt has the opportunity to see you. Let's be clear about one thing: I am not asking you to neglect rest because that is equally important. Society has created this idea of the grind mentality of only sleeping a few hours. The human body will only perform to what it is prepared for. What you don't want are diminishing returns because you're following a plan laid out by the latest influencer. You must define what early looks like to you and it is imperative that you find that rhythm. You can't stay up late running the town and then think you will be ready for the hunt. You have to be strategic and that means planning. Not just routine planning but planning with a purpose. You have to go forward with intent because you can't afford to miss another opportunity, or it will be a painful reckoning with the pride (the mirror, your future, your goals) afterwards.

Having The Strength To Go Back Out

So you've done the work. Now you have to trust the process. A friend of mine went on hunts for a few days and came back empty handed each time. We talked about what was happening and he said he felt he needed to make a few more adjustments to be sure he dotted all the i's and crossed all the t's. He mentioned everything from the type of deodorant he wore to the scent he'd spray on his clothes and even the route he was going to take to get back to his deer stand. Of all the things he told me, there was one thing that stood out the most. On this one particular day, he was late getting out there due to the rain. Instead of sitting home and doing nothing, he decided to go to the range to sight his rifle again. To his surprise, his rifle was firing off center and after a few strategic adjustments, he was shooting center mass. That adjustment would pay off a few hours later when he successfully came back home with the buck he'd been hoping for.

Had he not had the strength to go back out, he wouldn't have gotten his prize. He knew he did everything he needed to do and all he had to do was act. Don't be derailed by a few bad seasons. You must trust the process and know that there is something great for you on the other side.

63

Isolation

BEING ALONE IS one of the hardest things for people. We crave company. We crave attention. We are too afraid of being alone with our thoughts and we don't want to face our true selves. Isolation will remind you of what matters. Therefore, it is important to make time for yourself part of your routine. Whether you're hunting or not, alone time can build you.

Most people have never sat by themselves, yet there are some people who prefer isolation. They enjoy being alone. They thrive in the moments when there are no others around to distract them and they don't have to answer every beckoning call. We should learn from these people.

When you are alone, you can focus. You can not only seek peace but in seeking peace, you are able to find out much about yourself along the way.

Most people don't want to be alone because this is when you are forced to listen to your own voice. This voice will tell you how you truly feel. Your voice and your reflection are the most honest things you have. While working on my journey towards post-traumatic growth, I realized I used music as a way to drown out the thoughts in my mind. I vividly remember telling my counselor that I was scared to be alone with my thoughts. When I said those words for the first time, I realized I was running from isolation. I was running from my voice. I was running from my thoughts because I knew if I faced them, I would break.

But here's the thing: the break was what I needed. I needed to go to that dark and quiet place, and I needed to scream. I needed to yell. I needed to cry.

I needed to be silent so I could not only hear what I was feeling and saying to myself, but I needed to sit still to figure out what it was God was trying to say to me in the middle of all the chaos that was happening in my life. It doesn't matter who or what you believe in, there is a voice that will speak to you if you are willing to sit in isolation. If you would just be willing to go there.

We get so caught up in our distractions that we never give ourselves a full chance to heal. We cover our wounds so the world can't see them, but wounds need to breathe so they can heal. If you were to go to that place where you can sit and be free, you can air out what is going on inside of you and the healing can begin.

So many people are broken but are unwilling to get the assistance they need because they are too afraid of being alone. Well, in this case, if you aren't getting the help you need, you're already alone. Just because there are others physically around you doesn't mean you aren't alone. If you are going to elevate and live up to your true purpose, you are going to need to take care of everything that is happening internally so that you aren't carrying your yesterday into your tomorrow.

64

Destiny and Purpose

WHAT DO YOU feel you are purposed for? Rollo May defined destiny as "the design of the universe speaking through the design of each one of us." Our ultimate destiny is death, but before that, our destiny includes whatever we are to become while we are here. There are biological, psychological, and cultural influences when it comes to our destiny, and there are also the wills and desires of the human mind. What does destiny look like to you? Have you identified where you want to go?

"If one does not know to which port one is sailing, no wind is favorable." —Seneca

You need to know where you're headed and why you're going there. Your purpose should be the reason why you are going there. Aimlessly traveling is a waste of time but when you know you have a place to be, you are more willing to stay on course and more mindful of your surroundings.

If you don't know where you want to end up, it doesn't matter which direction the wind is blowing, you will simply end up wherever it takes you.

So many people have found themselves in a position where the wind has just been blowing them along and they're comfortable because they feel safe. They feel safe because they are surrounded by a sea full of people who are all doing the same things. They see other boats in the water with familiar faces so they feel they are in a good place. But eventually, the crowd will thin. The crowd will thin because as we navigate the waters of life, everyone will begin to face their own storms. The storms we face in life serve to shape us. Some storms will cause people to drift away from you. The winds of the storm will separate you from comfort. The winds of the storms will push you further away from familiarity. They will take you out of the calm waters where you feel nothing can go wrong and place you in the depths where the true tests begin. Some storms will overtake the unprepared and they will be capsized.

Smooth seas don't make skillful sailors. It is the one who is able to navigate through the chaos that rises to the top. It is the one who is able to withstand being tossed by the sea that endures and gets to their destiny.

What happens is most people never learn how to sail when the winds are favorable. They don't see the need. A lull in battle has the ability to blind the fighter into thinking all is well but fighting can erupt in an instant. The stillness of the water can fool a novice sailor the same way. The reality is you are either headed toward a storm, in a storm, or coming out of a storm. This is the way life works, and when it comes to chasing your goals toward purpose and fulfillment, if you truly want to get there, you will need to learn that life is about ships. As you navigate the waters of life, you need to know the role these ships play in your life.

65

Ships

Relationships

Some relationships last only for a season. Some relationships help you learn what not to do. Other relationships teach you what love is and how it is supposed to feel.

You will also need to understand your relationship with stress, happiness, self-love, doubt, and every other emotion because all of these, at some point in time, will affect every one of your ships.

Friendships

When you are young, having a long list of friends is desired. But as you age, you will have less desire to make friends because the number of true friends you have will diminish. It will diminish substantially when you make yourself a priority.

A focused mind doesn't leave time to entertain the crowd, therefore the need to please and hang out is no longer there as it was in your younger days .

There will be others who will support you in all of your endeavors and you will need their support because times will get tough and you will be blown off course. When that happens, you will need to leverage the relationships you have with friends to help you adjust your sails.

Leadership

You are the leader of your ship and in order to lead effectively, you need to know how to lead yourself first. This means you need to be ever aware of what is needed to become the better version of yourself. This means gaining a higher level of self-awareness and self-management. Knowing how you feel and what makes you tick is one thing and it is another to be able to manage it properly.

66

Purpose

YOU MAY LOOK at everything you have been through and think that you have been abandoned and you are lost, but there is a purpose in your pain if you look for it. It's not going to come to you right away. What you've gone through in your life isn't by chance. Sometimes the pain is necessary. Pain is nature's way of teaching and protecting us. Pain reminds us of what mistakes not to make again.

Sometimes things happen to slow you down. What you've gone through has built you up with a layer of armor that is impenetrable. It's meant to prepare you for battle. Every year you've cried and every lost night of sleep was to get you to where you are right now. The generals who are selected to lead troops in battle aren't selected just because they've studied war. They aren't put in command because of their time in service. Every one of them is strategically placed because they have shown they have what it takes. Just as they were chosen, so were you.

Who is it you want to become? If you were able to write that person's story, who would they be? You have the opportunity to create a version of you who has the ability to do anything in the world. You are only limited by what you can imagine yourself doing. You were called to a purpose and it is up to you to live it out.

Gone are the days of feeling as if you aren't worthy enough. You are more than adequate. You are beyond capable. You are the only person walking in your shoes. I don't care what past mistakes you've made or how many times you felt like giving up. None of that matters right now. The only thing that matters is whether you are willing to see it to the end. You're still alive. You have breath in your lungs and blood running through your veins. It is up to you to maximize it. It is up to you to put your foot on the gas and start heading towards your tomorrow.

There is a vision in you that only you can bring to the world. There is an invention with your fingerprint on it that can only be created by someone who has gone through what you've gone through. There's a story that only you can tell. Will you tell it? There's a song only you can sing. Will you sing it? There's a book that only you can write. Will you write it?

What will it take for you to walk into your glory? There is no greater time than right now for you to act on what you truly want.

67

F.P.R.N

Focused

It is time to focus. One of the most powerful things in the world is a light that is focused on a single point. With a magnifying glass, light from the sun is amplified and can cause paper to burn. Magnified light can become a laser strong enough to cut through some of the hardest materials there are. There is light in you, and in order for that light to shine to its full potential, you must become focused. It is the concentrated power of light into a single area that gives it strength. My best friend told me many years ago that he saw me operating all of my gifts but he saw it as a flood light that was illuminating them all. Although I was good at many things, he said to become great, I needed to narrow in from being a large flood of light, dabbling in art, music, drawing, leadership, and more, and focus on the thing that would give me fulfillment and was in line with my purpose. It took many years before I was able to dial that light down and since doing that, I've gone from just being focused to now being like a laser, bright and powerful. Now it's your turn.

Powerful

With the power that came from me walking in my purpose, I was able to lead like I had never led before. I became increasingly aware of my shortcomings and worked tirelessly to fix those things. I did this because the Marines I was leading and my family depended on me to be the best version of myself. By chasing perfection, I constantly improved in how I operated. I studied daily. I enrolled in college. I read books. I found people who were doing the things I desired to do and I identified everything they were doing that was good and fit with the image of myself I wanted to become. I got myself back on the potter's wheel. I started to reshape my thinking. I changed the way I responded when I was upset. I took a deeper look at my level of emotional intelligence and started to work on my shortfalls.

You must remember that when you have focus and you become powerful, your light can also be dangerous. Just as lasers can be used for good, focus and power can lead to you neglecting other things that matter so I was sure to consider my family in my journey. Managing the relationship with my family and the relationships I had with others was key.

I became relentless in my pursuit of personal greatness, and I am still on that road now. I am relentlessly chasing after being the man I dream of becoming. I am relentlessly pursuing beating the person I am today. I want to be able to look back at the person who wrote this book and say that I am light years beyond that. I will continue to push towards the mark of personal greatness and fulfillment because I am focused, I am powerful, I am relentless, and my time is now.

I want to leave an indelible mark on the heart of this world. One that echoes in history like the stoics of old. One that my children's children can be proud of. I am not fascinated with the idea of leaving wealth in just the financial form. Although I want them to be taken care of, leaving money as the only form of wealth is insufficient when you could have imparted knowledge, skills, values, morals, and vision as well. I want future generations to be able to turn the pages of this book and know that I poured my heart into it for the purpose of changing the mind of someone who was on the verge of giving up.

I want this book to be passed on to strangers on the first leg of flights and for them to pass it off to those they love. I want people to be able to see themselves achieving. I want people to feel as if they can go one more mile, one more day on the job, and one more day in the classroom. Again, it's about small daily contributions. When we master that, we will eventually get into a state of flow where everything is falling in line just the way it is supposed to.

There is a vision in every one of us and many times your vision is one that only you see. No one ever thought you'd be able to watch a movie on a cell phone. Not many people would have imagined electric vehicles. What great inventions do you have in your mind? What skill set do you have that can better humanity? What can you do that can better the person to the left and right of you? Whatever it is, start doing it now. No more waiting. No more procrastination. No more doubting. No more adding to your plate, it is time to eat what is on it! Get up and chase your dreams. It is time to get focused. You are powerful. Be relentless in execution because your time is now!

68

A Letter To You

MY BEAUTIFUL FRIEND,

Expect success as you pursue your goals, but not perfection. Revel in small victories, but don't expect to get it right every time. With each mistake comes an opportunity to learn, grow, and more importantly, the ability to see things through another lens.

Dr. Myles Munroe says that "sight is the ability to see things as they are, and vision is the capacity to see things as they could be." Don't let the reality of today stop you from seeing your true vision. Let your vision be the lighthouse that guides you as you work towards finding your purpose.

As you work towards your purpose, be kind to yourself. Be proud of the person that had the courage to get up and start over. Know that you are human and that it is perfectly acceptable to wonder if you're on the right track, but what's meant for you is for you. If you stay the course, one day all of your hard work will pay off.

In this very moment, you are positioned to change your life. It is time to align your actions with what your soul came to do. In order to do that, your behavior now must be consistent with your values. Everything you have gone through in your life up to this point was positioning you to be right where you are.

The world is waiting for you to erupt. Your gifts are waiting to erupt. You are that volcano that has been lying dormant but every day the rumbling can be felt. Every idea, every dream, and every action step is a shifting of the inner core. You possess a magnificent power and only you can bring it to light, so there is no more holding back.

May you have the strength to be on your way. May your destination become clear. May you have the will to act and may your journey towards elevation, purpose, and fulfillment be great.

I cannot wait to see what you accomplish.

I love you all and I wish the best as you elevate in your journey towards purpose and fulfillment.

Dimyas C. Perdue

By the way,

June 16, 2023,

my mom signed and

received the keys

to her new house.

Promise fulfilled.